Other books by Greg Vetter:

FIND IT IN 5 SECONDS:
GAINING CONTROL IN THE INFORMATION AGE

WINNING THE PRODUCTIVITY GAME

Greg Vetter

Copyright © 2016 by Greg Vetter

All rights reserved. No part of this book may be reproduced, scanned, or distributed in any printed or electronic form without permission.

First Edition: May 2016

Printed in the United States of America

ISBN: 978-0-9799071-1-1

Published in the U.S.A. by
Atlantic Productivity Press, Atlanta, Georgia
In partnership with Suncoast Digital Press, Sarasota, Florida

Dedicated to

Dr. Russ Osmond
Thank you for the rain.

Acknowledgments

I am very appreciative to the following for their assistance:

Barbara Dee at Suncoast Digital Press and Amy Collins at New Shelves.

John Vetter, Cheryl Lezovich, Kent Shaw, Murray Friedman, Vicki McCown, and Esther Creek.

David Greenberg, Doug Smart, Jeff Justice, Marty Suhr, Wes Wasson, Greg Adams, Henry Olner, Barry Zipperman, Abe Walking Bear Sanchez, Charles Reny, Philip Anderson, Ralph Edwards, Carol Hacker, Gregory Smith, Jansen Chazanof, Kelli Mejia, Wadie Hasweh, Bill Neill, Frank Payne, Patricia Hill, Taco Proper, Jill Hendon, Al Rossi, Karen Filz, Helen Royals, Bob Townsend, Graham Roberts, Paul Otte, Anthony Maida, Mike Stewart, Steve McClelland, Leslie Zigel, Linda Lindsey, Diann Guns, Bill Clunan, Tricia Malloy, Brian Lynch, Tom Cramer, Betsey Menneg, Joan Stewart, Alan Black, Tim Morrison, Fred Hartley, Dan Bateman, Wendell Prescott, Craig Kasold, Camden Clay, Jonathan Cohen, Rob Wilson, Rodney Johnson, Peter Chatel, Shawn Clark, Andy Linial, Paul Johnson, Fr. Greg Goolsby, Leslie Hunter, Shelia Haskell, Alan Epstein, Lynda Roth, Michelle Wilson, Terry Kingery, John Christensen, Eddie Huckaby, Lorene Sartan, Anita Liotta, Rich Newton, Neil Galanti, Ken Futch, Bruce Gaynes, Uwe Scherf, Renee Walkup, Lee Perrett, Loreli Robbins, Ken Levine, Tomas Ambrosetti, Lee Small, Loretta Waters, Tammy Bliss, Jeff Bach, Glenn van den Heuvel, Andy Dufek, and finally, Bob Cleland, Karen Price, Lee Ann Kleinfelter and Daniel Coburn.

Contents

Foreword xi
Introduction. xv
Tip 1.   There are three ways to improve your work output. 1
Tip 2.   Action creates energy. 2
Tip 3.   It takes more work to evade a task than to accomplish it. 2
Tip 4.   Doing something poorly is better than not doing it at all. 3
Tip 5.   Success is measured by what you complete, not by what you begin. . .3
Tip 6.   Make time from time that you don't think you have. 4
Tip 7.   One hour of uninterrupted time is equal to three hours of a regular day. . 4
Tip 8.   Be still and really listen. 5
Tip 9.   Listen like this. 6
Tip 10. Habits create needs. 6
Tip 11. Gear your behavior to be both goal-producing and tension-reducing. . .7
Tip 12. Slow down. 8
Tip 13. Process information only three times a day. 8
Tip 14. Produce work three times a day. 9
Tip 15. P six times a day. 10
Tip 16. Set up your day around your Quiet Time 11
Tip 17. Process before you Produce. 11
Tip 18. Everything you keep is either an Action or a Support. 12
Tip 19. Separate your Actions from your Support. 13
Tip 20. Keep Action items totally separate from your Support items. 13
Tip 21. Limit your technology. 14
Tip 22. Less effort creates more results. 15
Tip 23. Change one thing at a time. 15
Tip 24. Just say no. 16
Tip 25. If what you are doing isn't working, stop doing it immediately. 16
Tip 26. Have the right stuff. 17
Tip 27. Feel. Felt. Found. 17
Tip 28. Choose to be Powerful rather than a Victim. 18
Tip 29. Disconnect. 19
Tip 30. Limit your information sources. 20
Tip 31. Keep everything off the floor. 20
Tip 32. Keep your desk, credenza, floor, and walls totally paper-free. 21
Tip 33. Close your door. 21
Tip 34. Face any direction but the door. 22
Tip 35. Keep a clear pathway to your desk. 22
Tip 36. Set up your office like the cockpit of an airplane. 23
Tip 37. Set up a paperless office. 23
Tip 38. Do not save every e-mail. 24
Tip 39. Use the 80/20 rule for how much to keep. 25
Tip 40. At the beginning of the year, clean out all of your computer files. 25
Tip 41. At the end of the year, clean out your office. 26
Tip 42. The less you have, the more you will get done. 27
Tip 43. The main reason to save something is because you are going to use it. 28

Tip 44.	A Category is a grouping of similar or like things.	28
Tip 45.	Use the same system to store and access your information.	29
Tip 46.	Use the first word that comes to mind when naming a file.	30
Tip 47.	A Form is a Form is a Form is a Form.	30
Tip 48.	Your paper, e-mail, and computer file names should all match.	31
Tip 49.	If you listen, you will hear it.	32
Tip 50.	Create file shortcuts in Windows Explorer.	32
Tip 51.	Process your e-mail messages. Don't do them.	34
Tip 52.	Use an Inbox and an Outbox if you use paper.	34
Tip 53.	Everything goes into your desk Inbox first.	35
Tip 54.	From your desk Inbox, there are only four places information can go.	35
Tip 55.	Deciding rather than Doing is the key to your desk Inbox.	36
Tip 56.	Stand when you go through your desk Inbox.	37
Tip 57.	Have an Inbox on one side of your desk and an Outbox on the other.	37
Tip 58.	Tear off used pages from your legal pads.	38
Tip 59.	Open your Windows Explorer.	38
Tip 60.	Windows Explorer is the quickest and easiest way to find anything.	39
Tip 61.	Save e-mails that you reference to Windows Explorer.	40
Tip 62.	Drag your Support e-mails to Windows Explorer.	42
Tip 63.	Leave time open during the day to work.	42
Tip 64.	Understand the distinction between Working and Producing.	43
Tip 65.	Work from a balanced diet of tasks.	44
Tip 66.	Set up your four Action Categories in folders in your e-mail program.	45
Tip 67.	Set up the same four Action Categories in your file drawer as you have in your e-mail system.	46
Tip 68.	Stop with the lists.	47
Tip 69.	Use a 3 x 5 card to remind yourself of something you need to do.	48
Tip 70.	Create an electronic note card reminder in your e-mail program.	49
Tip 71.	Think Assembly Line when you work.	50
Tip 72.	Have a file called "Talk With" or "Discuss" in your Batched Category.	51
Tip 73.	Items that you are waiting for without a specific date go into Pending.	52
Tip 74.	Sent e-mail is different from Pending	52
Tip 75.	Stop assigning due dates to every task.	53
Tip 76.	E-mails can go only to one of four places: FADS.	54
Tip 77.	Completely empty your e-mail Inbox.	54
Tip 78.	E-mails to call on a date can be dragged to the Calendar.	55
Tip 79.	You can save an e-mail with its attachments to a specific date.	56
Tip 80.	Tasks which are too big to do can be made into Projects.	57
Tip 81.	Break your Projects into small pieces.	57
Tip 82.	80% of getting a Project done is setting up the Guide Sheet.	58
Tip 83.	Filling out the Guide Sheet is the key to accomplishing a Project.	59
Tip 84.	He who originates it, keeps it.	60
Tip 85.	Brevity communicates.	61
Tip 86.	Bite your tongue.	61
Tip 87.	Send a written Thank You note.	62
Tip 88.	Use a five step approach to speaking.	62
Tip 89.	Call people who like to listen. E-mail or text people who like to read.	63
Tip 90.	Cut down on clicks by making it a Favorite.	64
Tip 91.	Brush up your formatting with the Format Painter.	65
Tip 92.	Underscore the files you want to save.	65
Tip 93.	A version control.	66

Tip 94.	Back up right now on paper.	67
Tip 95.	Highlight the words that you need to work on.	69
Tip 96.	Save only the attachments from an e-mail.	69
Tip 97.	Delegate rather than work late.	70
Tip 98.	Keep only five things on your desk.	71
Tip 99.	Every loose paper on your desk is a decision not made.	71
Tip 100.	The less you have on your desk, the less you will be interrupted.	72
Tip 101.	Create boundaries in your life.	72
Tip 102.	Make a decision with every item on your desk.	73
Tip 103.	Keep your smartphone on the same spot on your desk.	73
Tip 104.	Ten things you should never, ever do with e-mail.	74
Tip 105.	Free e-mails that are being blocked.	75
Tip 106.	Change the heading names on your Sort by bar in Outlook.	75
Tip 107.	Answer with a repetitive e-mail response.	76
Tip 108.	Change e-mail attachments that were sent to you.	77
Tip 109.	Rename your e-mail messages when you save them.	77
Tip 110.	Use a different e-mail template for your coworkers.	78
Tip 111.	What goes around comes around.	79
Tip 112.	There are basically two reasons for using e-mail.	80
Tip 113.	Have the Ribbon area always visible on top.	81
Tip 114.	Know when to call and when to e-mail.	81
Tip 115.	Limit your Cc's.	82
Tip 116.	Reply with "Do I really need this?	82
Tip 117.	Standardize an e-mail template.	83
Tip 118.	Put an A or an S in the e-mail Subject line when someone is traveling.	84
Tip 119.	Take a stroll rather than a scroll.	85
Tip 120.	Include your name and phone number when sending e-mail.	86
Tip 121.	Set up a Signature for your e-mails.	86
Tip 122.	Forward an e-mail–the safe way.	87
Tip 123.	Scrolling = Producing nothing.	88
Tip 124.	Rules Schmules.	89
Tip 125.	Move all of your Support saved e-mails to Windows Explorer.	89
Tip 126.	Save your e-mails to Windows Explorer by using .msg.	90
Tip 127.	Create icons on your Quick Access Toolbar to save clicks.	91
Tip 128.	Use these icons on your Quick Access Toolbar.	92
Tip 129.	Use your To-Do Bar so your Calendar and appointments are visible.	93
Tip 130.	Keep an extra e-mail to manipulate by using a Bcc.	93
Tip 131.	Completely clean out your Inbox by creating a temporary one.	94
Tip 132.	Reply to your e-mail messages later.	95
Tip 133.	Save an e-mail with its attachments to a specific date.	96
Tip 134.	Stop incoming e-mail notifications from appearing on your screen.	96
Tip 135.	Edit your e-mails to include an action that you just took.	97
Tip 136.	See attachments easily.	98
Tip 137.	Tap your way into seeing your files on the Taskbar.	98
Tip 138.	Occasionally bigger is better.	99
Tip 139.	Create your very own Tab in Outlook.	99
Tip 140.	Set up your default.	100
Tip 141.	Use the Bottom Reading Pane when going through e-mail.	101
Tip 142.	Use the Right Reading Pane when working from your Action folders.	101
Tip 143.	Create shortcut icons for your software programs on your Taskbar.	102
Tip 144.	Rename the Subject line of an e-mail.	103

Tip 145.	Use the F12 key for when you need to use Save As.	103
Tip 146.	Using Search versus using a good filing system	104
Tip 147.	Color is the quickest and easiest way for you to organize anything.	104
Tip 148.	To the right, ever to the right.	105
Tip 149.	Keep a tax due date list..	106
Tip 150.	Use the date of service as the invoice number.	107
Tip 151.	Break down tax deductions by subject.	107
Tip 152.	All paper should be kept in only one room in your home.	108
Tip 153.	Junk your Junk Drawer.	109
Tip 154.	Keep a basket at the top and the bottom of the stairs.	109
Tip 155.	All household mail goes into your home Inbox.	110
Tip 156.	Got stuff?	110
Tip 157.	Every piece of paper has energy	111
Tip 158.	Read a page a day.	112
Tip 159.	Your Inbox will be with you for a long time.	112
Tip 160.	You are the biggest cause of your interruptions.	113
Tip 161.	It's time for a Time Out for your kids.	113
Tip 162.	Work on only one task at a time.	114
Tip 163.	How to stay focused on one task.	114
Tip 164.	Turn off all alerts, cues and vibrations on your devices.	115
Tip 165.	Know thy key activity.	116
Tip 166.	Important and Urgent are not the same.	116
Tip 167.	Your priorities stay the same.	117
Tip 168.	Prioritize, rather than Urgentize or Easinize your tasks.	117
Tip 169.	Be a fire marshal rather than a fire fighter.	118
Tip 170.	Many important tasks do not have a due date.	118
Tip 171.	If you have too much on your plate, tip it.	119
Tip 172.	Set up your day around your key activity.	119
Tip 173.	Work on your key activity first..	120
Tip 174.	Follow the flow.	120
Tip 175.	Leave ten minutes earlier for your morning commute.	121
Tip 176.	When you go on vacation, leave your troubles behind.	122
Tip 177.	Use yellow manila folders for paperwork to work on when traveling.	122
Tip 178.	Pack a box for each specific area when you move.	123
Tip 179.	Eliminate having to drive in bad traffic.	124
Tip 180.	Know where your sales come from.	125
Tip 181.	Reduce the number of products you sell.	126
Tip 182.	The 80/20 Rule: Your Sales Team.	126
Tip 183.	Use a checklist form to streamline your work processes.	127
Tip 184.	Lead with the model of having time.	128
Tip 185.	Set up a performance review every six months with your employees.	128
Tip 186.	Your assistant's productivity is directly proportionate to the amount of quality time you spend with that person.	129
Tip 187.	Manage your employees from a 3 x 5 card.	130
Tip 188.	Hire your missing skill..	130
Tip 189.	Cut all the dotted lines above below you in an org chart except one..	131
Tip 190.	Ask each of your employees what their Priority is.	131
Tip 191.	Set up a job description around a person..	132
Tip 192.	Hire someone who likes to change.	132
Tip 193.	Have your interviewee show you.	133
Tip 194.	Stop the meetings.	134

Tip 195.	The best facilitator for a meeting is someone other than the boss.	134
Tip 196.	Use meetings for decision-making and brainstorming.	135
Tip 197.	Stand during meetings.	136
Tip 198.	Standardize how you store information throughout your company.	136
Tip 199.	Combine as many forms as possible into one form.	137
Tip 200.	Repair a Microsoft Office problem.	137
Tip 201.	Fix the process.	138
Appendix 1: GLOSSARY.		141
Appendix 2: THE BIG PICTURE.		143
Appendix 3: PROCESSING AND PRODUCING.		144
Appendix 4: ACTION AND SUPPORT.		145
Appendix 5: SUPPORT CATEGORIES IN WINDOWS EXPLORER.		146
Appendix 6: FADS.		147
Appendix 7: OATS.		148
Appendix 8: ACTION CATEGORIES.		149
Appendix 9: ACTION CATEGORIES IN YOUR E-MAIL.		150
Appendix 10: 5 STEPS OF YOUR E-MAIL INBOX.		151
Appendix 11: 5 STEPS OF YOUR DESK INBOX.		152
Appendix 12: HOW THE *A VETTER WAY*® SYSTEM WORKS.		153
About the Author.		155
Products.		156
Programs.		157

Foreword

by Thomas S. Blackstock - Former Vice President
Supply Chain Operations Coca-Cola North America

It has been a number of years since my retirement from The Coca-Cola Company where I was responsible for all the company owned-manufacturing operations in North America but I am still haunted by the day-to-day stress of the job. Sometimes I wake up thinking I forgot to clear e-mails, or I missed an important meeting. A typical day in my work life was a barrage of voice mails, e-mails, texts and phone calls on top of a meeting agenda that pretty much consumed the day. Sometimes it felt like a good day was one where you simply had the time to get to all the meetings, clear your e-mails, voice mails, and phone calls and react to the critical communications. But, the company hired me to do more than that and I always knew in my heart that just getting through the day was not getting the job done.

Companies spend countless hours writing job descriptions describing the "real" job and these descriptions almost never include clearing e-mails, voice mails, texts and showing up at all the meetings as the primary job. The *real* job usually includes evaluation of business opportunities, analysis of metrics, problem identification and the development of actions plans. The *real* job almost always requires an extensive use of the mind to think through issues and apply past experience to plan the best way forward for the business. The *real* job may also require that one spend time with associates, coaching and developing the next generation of managers. The problem for today's employees, managers and organizations, given the inundation and barrage of all types of media, is how they can preserve and schedule the quality time required to get the *real* job done.

In the early 90's, Greg Vetter introduced me to a management system that promised to provide a solution to preserve and protect quality time for me and my entire organization. His system provided the methodology to sift through the bombardment of media and data, keep what was important, trash the garbage, and hold onto that which needed more investigation. At the heart of the system was developing the ability to clearly segregate the activity of *Processing* from the activity of *Producing*, and setting up the office to maximize production and minimize processing. For me it was easy to set up because I had the dedicated services of Greg and an administrative assistant that could be counted on to take over much of the processing activities. The real challenge was whether or not the organization was ready to receive such a system or not. Would they recognize the problems that impaired productivity in the workplace or would they reject the system as just another idea of the month?

The response from the organization was overwhelming. We set up an initial training program for the organization and the rest is history. Requests for additional training were constant. Most of the groups in the Atlanta home offices under my charge implemented the system. A laboratory in Columbus, Ohio chose to implement the system to manage lab records. I learned that everybody in the organization at every level of the organization had the same urge—everybody wanted to perform the *real* job better. Everyone had the sense that the media clutter of the workplace was a huge barrier, and that a standardized management system was a huge idea.

Over time managers retire, organizations change, and new people are hired, but the *A Vetter Way*® system lives on. My previous administrative assistant, Jocelyne Jones, is still a user of the system and she has trained a number of other administrative assistants and a few bosses on the system. There are numerous other committed users that still use the system. I am not sure that the system is still used by entire organizational units because people have moved on, but it probably should be or these organizational units are missing out on productivity improvements.

You have an exciting journey ahead should you engage the *A Vetter Way*® system. I have learned that it is a system—and like all systems, it has to be adopted as a whole. The elimination of a few components just because they are uncomfortable is a risk because all the components depend upon each other. I have also learned that the system requires discipline and without the discipline to stay committed to the system you will be back to where you started in a hurry. At first it is not easy, but over time it becomes a habit and is much easier.

Good luck with your journey on *A Vetter Way*®!

Thomas S. Blackstock

Former Vice President Supply Chain Operations, Coca-Cola North America

Introduction

You need to know you are playing a game. The game is to see how quickly and efficiently you can sift through endless amounts of incoming information so that you can do your real work.

Sadly, many of you aren't winning the game. Rarely do you spend quality time getting your real work done. But there is a way to win if you understand how to play.

You may feel your fiercest opponent is the clock. Some work does not get done on time, and some work never gets done. Sometimes, entire weeks go by with little or no time for critical thinking.

Second, you need to know the game is rigged. There is more information coming at you than you can possibly handle. Yet, you have been taught to believe that you should be able to handle the information overload instantly, continuously—and flawlessly! This, while doing the work of three people and satisfying the expectation to be available to your customers and others at any and all times.

Third, you are not aware of how much time you spend processing, that is, reviewing, checking, organizing, prioritizing, and categorizing all this information which continuously interrupts you. When you're interrupted and switch gears into processing, it means you stop producing work.

This distinction between processing information and producing work is vital. You may think that because you're answering e-mail, you are producing work. True, when you process information you may be working, but you are not necessarily producing work or results.

Your success is determined not by what you process, but by what you produce. That is what you're paid to do. You grow your career or your business not by processing information or answering e-mails, but by producing work!

However, you cannot simply ignore the need to process information any more than you can continue trying to process it as you always have. That just means longer work hours, taking work home, and feeling like you're always in the game.

The solution? A radically different way to work that enables you to win the productivity game.

I started Vetter Productivity and created the organizational system, *A Vetter Way*®, over twenty-five years ago. Through the years, I have had the good fortune to work with many brilliant, successful people across the country; from presidents to secretaries, in one-man businesses to Fortune 50 companies, in educational institutions, government agencies, and non-profit organizations. Each person whom I've worked with contributed to refining and improving my system. This book captures all this refinement of the last quarter century in bite-sized, doable tips.

These tips are exactly what they say they are—time-saving solutions to work smarter, faster and easier. Start anywhere, choose only those tips that you want to do, those you can see the benefit of doing. There is nothing harder than trying to change something you don't want to change because you think it's what you're supposed to do.

Working in the change business has shown that most of us attempt to change too many things at once. Instead, simply work on only one tip at a time. Get it down as a habit before you start on the next one.

Change is challenging! Each tip will challenge you to change, so keep in mind that unless you want the same stress and chaos many people experience at work today, things must change. Truth is, if you don't feel uncomfortable, overwhelmed, uncertain, or confused, you probably aren't changing anything. The good news is that this book will teach you systems, methods and new actions that are proven, so no guessing or struggling is involved in finding the best ways to save time and produce results.

As with any game, remember to make this one fun also. I find it is way more fun to produce results quickly and easily. It's fun to learn new things which are instantly helpful, and it is fun to have a growing sense of achievement and accomplishment. Something prompted you to pick up this book of game-changing tips, so you are already on your way to a more successful and fun path to winning the productivity game. Good luck!

WINNING THE PRODUCTIVITY GAME

201 Time-Saving Solutions to Work Smarter, Faster and Easier

1

There are three ways to improve your work output.

Do you ever wonder if you are working as productively as possible? Heading back to the office from the golf course right now might be a good start.

Here are three ways to check:

1. Your Focus – Are you working on the correct thing? (Few people do. They work on what they like to do or are comfortable doing, not on what they really need to do.) What is that one, correct thing that you always need to be working on?

2. Your Methodology – Do you have a good system of working? (Many people don't use a real system while others use a system they picked up along the way and kind of modify it as they go along.) What system do you use?

3. Your Speed – Do you work faster than a normal worker would in order to keep up? (Ouch! Nobody wants to work fast all of the time. It is exhausting and after a while you'll get sick.) Are you able to work at a comfortable and steady pace?

What many workers do today is simply work more hours rather than fix the problem. Some, believe it or not, actually take work home and are available 24 hours a day to respond to e-mails, calls, and texts, wherever they are.

Hey! Forget about working more hours and working crazy.

Instead, stay focused on that one thing and use a better, make that a Vetter, work system.

2

Action creates energy.

How do you feel when you just sit around for days? Tired? Lethargic? Now compare that with how you feel after working out.

When you feel stuck, do something, do anything. The mere act of doing something causes you to create energy, which in turn allows you to do other things. It's as if you are creating a source of fuel for yourself when you take some kind of action.

Think about grilling a steak. The steak doesn't stop cooking just because you pull it off of the fire. It continues to cook from the energy created by the movement of the heated molecules. That's why your Medium-Rare steak mysteriously turns into a Medium later on.

The same is true for you. Do nothing and, well, nothing happens.

Don't make a Mistake. Be Rare! Do something Well Done!

3

It takes more work to evade a task than to accomplish it.

Do you know that you spend more energy avoiding doing something than just going ahead and doing it?

Think how much time you have spent (or more appropriately wasted) throughout the years "thinking about" tasks that you needed to do. If the time you spent "thinking about" those tasks counted as work completed, every task you ever wanted to do in the last twenty years would have been completed about, oh, nineteen years ago.

The next time you realize you are starting to "think about" something you need to do, just shift gears and start doing it.

The job will be done before you know it.

Now get started!

4

Doing something poorly is better than not doing it at all.

How many times have you avoided working on something because you were concerned about how well you would do it? What kind of result did you get when you didn't do anything? Exactly!

Accomplishing a task with an average result—or for that matter, even a poor one—sure beats the heck out of no result at all.

Some result is always better than no result.

It's a hard one to learn.

5

Success is measured by what you complete, not by what you begin.

How many items on your to-do list have you begun but never have seemed to be able to finish?

Back in 1984, I started selling telephone systems, door to door, competing against the telephone company. (Back then, there was only one Phone Company and boy, was that a hard sale!)

On one Friday, my sales manager called me into his office as to the number of phone systems I had sold for the week. I proudly replied that I had delivered an unprecedented 12 sales proposals. After commenting that it was great that I had 12 proposals out, my manager again asked me how many I had closed. Gulp!

Working on a lot of things is admirable. The secret to success, however, is getting your work completed.

Finish one, before you begin another one.

6

Make time from time that you don't think you have.

How many times have you said, "I don't have time to do that?"

If you were guaranteed a million dollars, would you have time then? Of course you would. Why then, and not before? Because with the million, you were able to see such a big payoff.

A way to shift from a victim mentality to a mentality of power is to say, "I choose to do something else" rather than "I don't have the time." It's subtle, but there is a difference.

Make time every day for your Quiet Time where you brainstorm, plan, think, improve, and drive your business—all of the things you don't seem to have time to do now.

Is it possible that you are not seeing the big payoff that is right in front of you?

As Ty would say to Danny in Caddyshack: "See—the payoff Danny. Be—the payoff. Nah, nah, nah, nah, nah, nah, nah."

7

One hour of uninterrupted time is equal to three hours of a regular day.

Guess what every administrative assistant would love to have—besides a big fat juicy raise. An hour a day when everyone would just leave them alone.

Oh, the work they could produce! You have the opportunity most of the time to do this but are probably blowing it.

I know, I know. You don't have the time. Well, no one else does either. But why choose to let that get in your way?

To win the Productivity game, you must create time from time (your Quiet Time) that you don't think that you have but which of course, you really do have.

Just ask your admin how valuable an uninterrupted hour is—and what they would give to get one.

Now please go to your room and be Quiet.

8

Be still and really listen.

Have you noticed that people just don't seem to be listening like they used to?

Do any of these sound familiar?

    a. While on the phone, you hear the faint clicking of typing in the background or the rustling of papers.

    b. While someone is talking to you, they look down at their smartphone more often than a kid on a car trip looking out of the window asking "Are we there yet?"

    c. They look at the sky or into la-la land while saying "Uh-huh" every five seconds, having absolutely no clue—none whatsoever—as to what you are talking about.

    d. After hearing your first sentence, they immediately start formulating what they will say to counter what you just said and from then on, interrupt you silly.

    e. Their smartphone rings and without saying anything—not even "Excuse me" or "Would you mind if I take this call?"—immediately start talking as if you weren't there. (Walking away when they do this is a riot. Some people notice—others don't.)

Most people just want to be heard. Don't you?

Try saying nothing and just being with someone. It's called listening.

The effect of listening is amazing—to you, to them, and to your bottom line.

9

Listen like this.

When someone says, "I need you to listen to me," how do you listen? (If it is your wife, you run. Oh wait, that's "We need to talk.")

a. Keep doing what you are doing, nod your head and tell them you are listening.

b. Say uh-huh every time they pause. Uh-huh.

c. Constantly interrupt them with unsolicited advice such as "Here's what you really need to do be doing, Hoss."

Hard to believe but there are other options. What about asking them how they would like to be listened to? Here are three ways to listen:

a. Passive listening: Just listen and say nothing. Most people just want to be listened to.

b. Active listening: Listen to what they are saying and then when they are done, tell them what you heard. ("What I heard you say was…") They will correct you if you didn't hear them.

c. Listening and advising: Listen to what they say and when they are done, make suggestions.

If you just want to be listened to, the very last thing you want to hear is advice.

How many times have you ever heard someone ask "How would you like me to listen?" I am guessing never.

Uh-huh.

10

Habits create needs.

Have you ever smoked a cigarette after a meal? For some reason, it is supposed to be really satisfying. Now I have never smoked a single cigarette so I am probably the last person on earth to be commenting on this but what the heck, I will anyway.

People who smoke always seem to really enjoy a cigarette after a meal. How come? My guess is they saw someone doing it so they innocently started. After a while, they got into the habit of smoking, which created the need for a cigarette. Now, a meal doesn't seem quite the same without one.

There is no difference between this habit and the habit of working your organizational system. If you repeat an action long enough, you will create the need for it.

The next time you want to make a change in your life, simply start doing a new action. Then do it again and again and again. Before you know it, you will have created the need to do that action. Now it is easier to do because you created a habit.

This, of course, applies to everything except doing your taxes.

11

Gear your behavior to be both goal-producing and tension-reducing.

Are you constantly engaging in activities that only reduce your tension? If you are, have you ever wondered why you aren't getting more results?

With every activity you get to choose: reduce tension or produce work.

Fortunately, with some activities, you're able to do both, such as working out at the gym. You reduce your tension level and build a strong, healthy body at the same time.

Why then, would you continue to waste your precious time with only tension-reducing activities?

The next time you reach for that bag of potato chips (munch), plop down in front of the TV (veg) or sip on another brewski (gulp or should that be chug?), you just may want to ask yourself what you're producing.

Hopefully, it's not just fat.

12

Slow down.

What's the rush?

Have you noticed you don't have enough time to get everything done? Guess what? You're not supposed to. Why are you buying into the belief that you are?

Why this obsession with always having to be busy, to be on the go, to be doing something? What are you afraid of missing? Or do you know that if you stay so busy, you won't have time to feel that deep hurt inside that you don't want to feel.

Being busy doesn't always mean being productive. It can also mean being exhausted, compulsive, mechanical, addicted, and joyless. Worse yet, it can mean not dealing with issues in your life. If you are always busy, you never have time to feel.

Isn't it finally time to slow down and feel what you have always been afraid to feel?

To feel is to heal.

13

Process information only three times a day.

How many times a day do you check your e-mail? Today an average person checks an electronic device 150 times in 24 hours. Hi, boys and girls. Can you say "interruption"? I knew you could.

Processing information consists of prioritizing, categorizing, sorting, organizing, and deciding. It is never, ever doing. Real work is never accomplished by Processing information (e-mail, voice mail, texts and Inbox) even though many workers believe that they are Producing work when they are opening, looking at, and forwarding texts and e-mails. Perhaps they are working but many times aren't Producing.

Go through and Process all incoming information three times a day—first thing in the morning, (before you start work or attend one of those wonderful and fulfilling meetings), after lunch, and finally late in the afternoon.

By the way, doing this means eliminating multitasking (Producing work and Processing information at the same time) from your day.

Process information only three times a day and watch your Productivity skyrocket.

♬ Skyrockets in flight. Morning, lunch and afternoon Processing delight. ♬

14

Produce work three times a day.

How many times a day do you have to stop and think what you need to do next? Imagine having a work system that thinks for you, keeps you on track, and allows you to Produce a lot more work.

Producing is creating results and accomplishing work. It's what you're paid to do. It's the opposite of Processing (sorting, categorizing, and prioritizing) information. Every day, Produce by working on each of your Action Categories:

- Batched – similar tasks that can be worked on and done together. Think of an assembly line.
- Calendar – tasks that can only be done today, or on a certain date, or in a certain month. Do not put tasks that are due in the future in here.
- To Do – Important and impactful tasks that you never seem to do. Tasks that have a due date that can be done before their due date. A step of a Project. Do these in your (QT) Quiet Time every day.

When you Process, Process. When you Produce, only Produce.

Doing these three, will make you free.

15

P six times a day.

Do you have a specific work system that you follow? How about a system for checking incoming information?

Many workers spend their day jumping back and forth between checking e-mails, replying to them, answering their phone, texting someone, going to meetings, and, in between all of this, trying to get some work done. If you don't have a specific system, chances are that you will be reacting to the urgencies of the day rather than pro-acting on what is important.

Break your day down into Processing information three times and Producing work three times.

- Process (Voice mail, e-mail Inbox, smartphone, and desk Inbox) First thing in the morning.
  - Produce (Calendar – tasks that can only be done on a certain date)
  - Produce (Batched – similar tasks that can be done together)
- Process (Voice mail, e-mail Inbox, smartphone, and desk Inbox) Lunchtime.
  - Produce (To Do – important and impactful tasks you work on in your Quiet Time)
- Process (Voice mail, e-mail Inbox, smartphone, and desk Inbox) Late afternoon.

By having a system and following a system, you, rather than your day, will be in control.

It's as easy as P'ing six times a day.

16

Set up your day around your Quiet Time

How much critical thinking or planning time do you spend during the day? How much?

Take 20% of your work day (the 80/20 rule) and spend it in a Quiet Time. A QT is an uninterrupted time when your door is shut and you are totally unplugged. That means surviving without your e-mail, smartphone, or cell for a short time. You will actually get a lot of work done without the constant interruptions. Imagine that.

Work on important and impactful tasks, tasks due in the future which can be done now, on steps from a Project, and on tasks that you have never have made time to work on before.

Create a block of time from time that you generally don't think you have. In other words, make the time to do your QT every day. Set up your day around your QT instead of trying to fit your QT in at the end of the day. It won't fit.

In one to three months you will be amazed when you have time to work on important tasks that you never seemed to have time to work on before.

There is absolutely nothing you can do during the day that is more important than this to increase your productivity.

17

Process before you Produce.

When you first get to work each morning, how often do you immediately start working on a task without checking your voice mail, e-mail, or Inbox contents? Doesn't it feel a little unnerving not knowing what surprises may rear their ugly and urgent head when you don't check them?

Process (categorize, prioritize, decide, sort, organize) all new information before you begin to Produce (do the work) work.

Processing gives you complete awareness and control of your day (at least the illusion of it).

The only surprises you really want are the ones on your birthdays.

18

Everything you keep is either an Action or a Support.

Do you remember the two kinds of energy from your General Science class?

One was Kinetic and the other was Potential. Here are some of the characteristics of Kinetic energy which we will call an Action and Potential energy which we will call a Support:

Properties of an Action	Properties of a Support
Kinetic energy (active)	Potential energy (possible)
A task to do	Something you want to save
An activity	Information that is stored
A verb is used with it	A resource
Intend to do it…now or in the future	No intention of doing anything with it

Everything you keep is either something you want to work on (Action), or information you want to save (Support) and be able to reference. If it is neither of these, you shouldn't have it as it will be trash to get rid of, or something that needs to go to someone else.

When all of your Action is stored in the same location, it is easy to know exactly what you need to work on since everything will be in that one spot. The same is true of the information you save. Everything you choose to save will be in one location (Category folder) broken down by a common subject.

"To be (Action) or not to be (Support). That is the question."

19

Separate your Actions from your Support.

Are tasks you need to work on mixed in with information you save and refer to? Or simply put, is everything in one big pile on your desk or everything saved in your e-mail Inbox?

Nine out of ten people can't tell the difference between an Action and a Support—even though they think they can. Tasks to work on (Action) are often stored with reference materials (Support).

Think about all the e-mails in your Inbox you need to work on that are mixed in with other e-mails on which you are waiting for something from someone else that are mixed in with e-mails you are just storing there because you don't know what to do with them. Whew!

The goal is to use the same Action system for your paper and your e-mail. Action is anything you intend to work on now or in the future—no matter when. The key in recognizing an Action is to listen for a verb when you have a thought. An intention of doing something with it. Support is information that you simply refer to with no intention of working on. Kind of like that chore your wife has repeatedly asked you to do.

By storing all of your Actions together in one spot, you will never forget what you need to work on.

80% of being organized is understanding the difference between an Action and a Support.

20

Keep Action items totally separate from your Support items.

Have you ever taken a legal pad to a meeting, written down meeting notes, and then written tasks that you need to do all on the same page?

Where do you keep the pad when you get back to your office? How do you store the meeting notes and then remember to work on the tasks you noted if they are both on the same page?

Always separate Action (anything you intend to work on now or in the future) from Support (information that you simply reference).

During a meeting, write notes on a legal pad or type them in your computer. Write tasks to be done on 3 x 5 cards or create an electronic New Post in This Folder reminder card in Microsoft Outlook.

That way when you come back from your meeting, you can file your meeting notes in your Support Categories and file the tasks you need to work on in your Action Categories.

Legal pads beware! Your numbers will soon be shrinking.

21

Limit your technology.

How many different ways do you want to be accessible? Usually one will work.

The more ways someone can reach you, the less work you'll get done. Let's break down the cycle:

1. The more technology you have, the more information sources you will have.
2. The more information sources, the more things that will interrupt you and the more things you will need to check.
3. The more you check (Process the information), the less you will get done (Produce work).

Technology is great if it is limited, learned, and utilized properly. No doubt that one state-of-the-art chainsaw is worth ten different types of axes—as long as you know how to use it properly.

Can you combine your technology?

Sometimes less really is more.

22

Less effort creates more results.

Have you ever tried swimming against a rip tide in the ocean?

If you have, you know it is a losing battle. The more you try to swim straight in towards shore, the more exhausted you get. The simple fact is the ocean is a lot stronger than you are, and there is a lot more of it than you. Sound like anything you are up against in your work life?

Rather than trying to fight the pull, why not harness the power to get you where you want to go—in this case, the shore.

As the rip tide takes you out to deeper water—exactly where you don't want to go—rather than panic, realize that this is part of the natural order of doing less and achieving more. Then swim diagonally in toward shore using the strength of the current.

Land ho!

Isn't it time that you started to work smarter, rather than harder?

23

Change one thing at a time.

How many resolutions do you make for the New Year? If you are like most people probably a bunch. How many do you keep? Well…that's another story.

Imagine what would happen if you focused all of your energy on changing just one aspect of yourself. What a far cry that would be from your annual attempt of the multitude of nearly unattainable goals you hope to accomplish with each New Year.

Once that singular change became a habit and you no longer had to remember to do it (don't believe it only takes 21 days), then, and only then, would you start on your next change.

What a refreshing change that would be, to actually uh…change.

Happy New Resolution!

24

Just say no.

Don't you just love being solicited on the phone for a donation?

You want to say yes but you already gave at the office and for that matter, everywhere else.

My favorite is: "We are collecting money for your local law enforcement agency. (It always feels as if not getting that sticker increases your chances of being pulled over and ticketed.)

Normally, when asked to contribute, you politely say "No Thank You." No longer. The next time someone calls, and asks, simply say…"No." That's it, just "No." A deafening quiet will follow with the caller not quite sure of what they just heard. It feels weird to just say no but it feels so powerful. Almost as if you actually had a say in your own life.

How many times have you said yes to someone this week when what you really wanted to say was no?

Say it now with me: "No."

25

If what you are doing isn't working, stop doing it immediately.

Are you happy with the way things are at work?

Didn't a famous author write that we are living lives of quiet desperation—which includes our work life?

That can change if you are willing to change but there is a catch. You really do have to change.

Do you remember the Seinfeld episode when George decided to do everything the opposite way because his life wasn't working? He saw a tall, beautiful woman in the restaurant. Normally he wouldn't think of approaching her but the new George did. As he walked up to her, he said, "Hi my name is George. I don't have a job…and I live with my parents." Of course the woman was immediately interested in him. Just the opposite of what he thought would happen considering his current belief system.

George knew what he was doing wasn't working. He didn't just talk about changing like most of us do, he actually changed his behavior.

Many of us really believe that we change our behavior.

Actually, we really don't.

The way you know you have changed your behavior is when you get a different result.

George is back, baby! And so are you if you really change what you are doing.

26

Have the right stuff.

Why do you have so much stuff? Or rather, why do you have so much stuff you don't need or use?

What are you missing in your life that you need and aren't getting? Take a few minutes to answer this very important question. Few people will. Instead they will continue to mindlessly buy, gather, and collect.

We often need something and don't know what it is. Then we try to fill that need with something else. Many times that something else clogs up our life and causes us to spin out of control—again and again and again.

Identifying what you really need is 80% of your solution.

27

Feel. Felt. Found.

Have you ever had to call the cable company because your cable was out? After waiting for what seemed like an eternity (it was), a customer disservice rep finally got to you.

Winning the Productivity Game

It had been days since you had service and the state of your mental health was becoming questionable. You were about to flip out, rather than flip through, your channels. After stating what the problem was, the cable company told you that you couldn't possibly be right, and then started to argue with you.

Not the kind of kid glove treatment you were hoping for.

If one of your customers ever calls and is unhappy, listen intently to what they are saying. Agree with what they are saying and acknowledge what they are feeling. When you do this, notice how quickly and easily the situation clears up. Here is a technique to use:

- "I understand how you Feel…" (I hear you. I get how you feel. You have a right to feel that way. I would be upset too!)
- "I Felt the same way…" (I understand. I get it. I was in the same boat as you are.)
- "What I Found out was…" (It turned out okay for me and it will for you too!)

It's an old sales technique that can be used in any situation. People just want to be heard, listened to, and acknowledged.

Customers do. Employees do. Don't you?

28

Choose to be Powerful rather than a Victim.

Is your boss a real doofus? I am sure a few of my old employees thought theirs was.

Years ago, I worked with an admin who gave a new meaning to the word victim. She seemed to believe her main job was to whine about how bad her boss was.

When she started on a new whine, I held up two fingers in the shape of a V. Inquiring as to what I was doing, I answered the V stood for victim and that was what she was doing again, being a victim. After that, you can imagine who was added to her "whine list" and it sure wasn't a French Bordeaux.

After arguing that her boss was clueless, I told her I agreed. She tilted her head quizzically as I experienced a silence rarely heard anywhere near her.

I explained that she wasn't forced to work for her boss. He was a real doofus but she did have a choice. If she stayed, she needed to understand her part in the dance that was going on and what she needed to do to make it work. Or, she could just leave and find a healthier job. Imagine that… but then, no justification to whine.

In a time of history imbued with such a strong sense of entitlement—that some people are owed something by everyone else—it might be a perfect opportunity for all of us to step up to the plate and actually choose to be responsible and accountable for our own lives.

'Nuff said.

29

Disconnect.

Have you ever wondered if you were a technology addict? Can you walk more than a couple of feet without having to call someone? Can you stop at a light without having to check your phone? Once in bed, can you go through the night without having to check your smartphone on your nightstand?

An addiction is an activity you can't stop doing. People can be addicted to many things—alcohol, drugs, gambling, TV, religion, sex, you name it. They can also be addicted to being "connected."

If you feel a compulsion to constantly check your iPhone, e-mail or anything else that gives you a buzz, you may have a challenge ahead.

Try this: After work, turn off your computer, tablet, and smartphone—anything that causes you to be connected. Just do it for one night. If you can't, it may be time to call Houston and tell them you have a problem.

As time goes on, addictions become worse…not better. The need for a greater fix increases until eventually you can never get enough and you can't stop.

Now is the time to stop before it gets out of control.

Just pull the plug and smell the flowers. Your life is already going by faster than you realize.

Don't speed it along any quicker.

30

Limit your information sources.

Have you ever stopped to think of all the different ways that you receive information?

It used to be simple—phone calls, paper, manila folders and pink "While you were out" messages in your Inbox. Then came the Information Age. E-mail was a wonderful way to send a memo to a large group—but somehow got out of control and was used as a phone. Instant messaging was a way to interrupt someone you couldn't reach because they were busy using e-mail. Shrewd! Smartphones combined e-mail with calendars, phones, cameras, and then you name it. Next Twitter, Facebook, and Instagram.

Tell me again how much more work you are getting done.

As Clint would say, "A man has got to know his limitations."

Do you know yours?

31

Keep everything off the floor.

How much stuff do you have strewn on your office floor? How about on your floors at home? Should I even ask about your basement or garage?

One of the first rules my father taught me when I worked in his construction business was to always keep the floor completely clean. That meant even sweeping up the sawdust. Come-on dad, sawdust? Yup.

Why keep your floors clean? So you can move quickly without having to think where to step or what to avoid stepping on, thus avoiding a costly accident.

How much time do you lose stepping around stuff on the floor? Isn't it time you made a decision as to what to do with all of that stuff?

Thanks, Dad! You were so much wiser than I ever realized.

32

Keep your desk, credenza, floor, and walls totally paper-free

Do you believe that if you can't see something, you'll forget where to find it?

If so, ask yourself this question: "Do I wear underwear?" If you do, then your underwear must be stored out where you can see it—either on a chair or on your bureau. It could never be hidden away in a drawer. Why? Because if you kept your drawers in a drawer, you could never remember where they were.

You can remember the whereabouts of your drawers because you have developed the habit of finding them and (hopefully) putting them on. The same type of habit can be developed to store your files out of sight in your file drawers, keeping your desk, credenza, and floor free from distractions.

If you follow the system of Producing work three times a day (important tasks, batched tasks, tasks that can only be done today) you will always know what to work on. Simply open your file drawer and there it is.

Remember, drawers in a drawer.

33

Close your door.

Does your company's culture dictate that your door be kept open?

I know, I know. It's antisocial and it goes against some company's culture to close the door, but so what? What's more important to your company? An open door with you constantly being interrupted (I don't even want to think about what an open door means to someone with ADD) or a closed one with more work being accomplished?

Everyone will still love you if your door is shut as long as you go to lunch with them once in a while—and pick up the check.

Warning: Let your coworkers know beforehand that you will be closing your door and why, or they really might think you don't love them.

34

Face any direction but the door.

If your desk is facing the door and someone walks by, what do you think the chances are of you looking up to see who it is?

I know, Mr. Feng Shui (and Tony Soprano) say to never have your back to the door. But come on, this is corporate America. If you think the enemy is going to sneak up on you, are you really working at the right place?

What will sneak up on you are the thousand times you will be interrupted when you look up to see who just walked by.

Besides, if anyone tries to sneak up on you, you can see their reflection in your computer monitor.

Boo!

35

Keep a clear pathway to your desk.

Do you have to turn slightly or watch where you step just to get to your desk?

Think about the width of a doorway. The opening is usually at least 30 inches wide. There's a reason—so you don't have to turn your body to fit through it.

The same is true about getting to your desk. You need an unobstructed pathway of at least 30 inches to be able to easily glide through to that comfy chair of yours.

Every twist, turn, and extra step will cause you to spend more time at the office, and we know how much you like that.

Time to clear that path. Timber!

36

Set up your office like the cockpit of an airplane.

How would you feel if your pilot had to stand up to flip a switch in order to land safely? Suddenly riding a train would sound a lot more desirable—and a lot safer.

The more you have to move, twist, turn, and walk in your office, the less you'll get done. Precious time is wasted when you have to stand and walk across the room to retrieve something or turn around to make a call or use your computer.

Work from one spot with your phone and computer on your desk.

"Ladies and gentleman, prepare to increase your productivity."

37

Set up a paperless office.

Have you ever considered going paperless in public? Sounds rather shocking, doesn't it?

You may want to if the majority of your information is electronic and you can scan the rest into your computer.

Two storage places are needed: One for tasks that you intend to work on (Action) and the other for information you want to save

Winning the Productivity Game

and refer to (Support). The suggested places we will be using are Outlook and Windows Explorer.

Store your tasks (Action) in your e-mail program. Simply drag the e-mails you need to work on to one of your Action file folders you created in the left Folder Pane window.

Store information (files or e-mails) you refer to and save (Support) in one of your Support Category folders under My Documents in Windows Explorer.

If you are unable to store Support information in My Documents, you have the option of saving it in your e-mail program. If you do, make sure you save all of your Support information from My Documents in your e-mail program so you only have one place to look rather than two.

Go ahead. Be daring. Go paperless in public!

38

Do not save every e-mail.

What percentage of your e-mails do you save?

Sadly, some workers believe they are supposed to save every e-mail that is sent to them. And if not every, almost every one.

Why?

- They are afraid to say they don't have it if asked by someone for it.
- They are afraid they will look unprofessional if they can't produce it.
- They don't trust their decision making ability.

Here are a couple of daily situations that occur and what to do with them:

When you are Cc'ed:

- Read it.
- Do not respond to it (your name was not under the To)
- Delete it.

Whenever possible, ask to be taken off of a Cc list when you can.

When you are asked a question:
- Reply to it.
- Delete it.

You can't save everyone (or for that matter, every e-mail that you receive).

39

Use the 80/20 rule for how much to keep.

Do you realize that you only use two out of every ten pieces of information in your computer or file drawer?

Here is the breakdown:

10	Computer, paper, or e-mail files.	100%
2	Files you actually use.	20%
6	Files you can delete or trash.	60%
2	Files you can store on a shared drive, Central Departmental File or Archive	20%

The less you have to handle, the more you will get done.

Pretty simple.

40

At the beginning of the year, clean out all of your computer files.

Have you ever heard, "Now there's a sloppy computer?"

Maybe a sloppy desk, but not computer. Many computers are a lot more disorganized than desks, yet somehow they never seem to be picked on. Well your time is up, computers.

To avoid "Sloppy Computer Syndrome," follow this easy process to clean out all of your computer files annually.

1. Type in all of your Support Category folder names in Windows Explorer under My Documents just like you had them before, except the new folders will be empty and have an underscore in front of them. Using an underscore such as _Clients, will move the folder to the top of the page, above your old Support Category folders and various other files you have collected and stored there. These new Support Category folders will be where you will save your new files and e-mails as well as the old ones below after you review and move them up.
2. As you open files that are stored in your old Support Category folders, simply save them under one of your new Support Category folders.
3. All of the files that you no longer use will be left in your old Support Category folders at the end of the year when you get to do this wonderful exercise again. Eventually, you'll want to delete all the files that you never opened.

I bet you are counting the days until you get to do this again next year.

41

At the end of the year, go through and clean out your office.

Are you aware that at the end of the year, your paper, e-mail and computer files desperately need to go on a diet? Over the course of the year, they have accumulated quite a few unnecessary pounds.

The goal is to make a decision on whether to: give the file to someone, take action on it, trash it or keep it. (Outbox, Action, Trash, Support) The worst thing you can do is ignore it and let it sit there and get bigger and bigger each year. Kind of like you did last year with it.

Questions to ask while you are enjoying this most entertaining of all possible activities:

- Is the information on my computer? (Why have a paper duplicate?)
- Have I looked at it this year? (Is the paper starting to parch?)
- Will or can someone keep this for me? (Information flows downward-sorry!)
- Can I store this in the central file or shared drive? (Let the lawyers/CPAs worry about it.)
- Does my Retention schedule require that it be saved? (Off it goes!)

Information is doubling and so probably is the size of your files while you are reading this. I know—what a great way to spend your Christmas vacation but it'll be well worth it when you walk into your clean and organized office next year.

Sometimes Slim should be something other than a cowboy's name.

42

The less you have, the more you will get done.

Remember when you were a kid and you'd leave your toys outdoors in the middle of winter and never think twice about them?

Now think about your beautiful car and golf clubs. Feel the same way now?

Quite simply, the more stuff you have, the more potential problems, and the more stuff you have to worry about.

The same is true in your office. How many e-mails do you have in your Inbox? How much paper is piled around your office?

How much more focused would you be if you got rid of all that stuff? It's weighing you down mentally, physically, and energetically.

Isn't it time to send all of that stuff to a galaxy, far, far away?

43

The main reason to save something is because you are going to use it.

How many times a day do you wonder if you should save something? A gazillion?

When you are looking at an e-mail or handling a piece of paper and you hear yourself saying any of the following words, immediately stop what you are doing and delete it or throw it away:

1. Might
2. May
3. Possibly
4. Could
5. Maybe
6. What if
7. Someday
8. Perhaps
9. You never know
10. You can never tell
11. In case of
12. Who knows

Your inability to get rid of anything is directly related to your fear of making a decision (or perhaps a mistake).

Isn't it time to start making more decisions?

P.S. You will never delete or throw anything away that is really valuable.

44

A Category is a grouping of similar or like things.

Do you know how your brain stores information?

The easiest way to store and find information is by using a Category. A Category is a grouping of similar or like items focused around a particular subject.

You already know how the Category model works—it's everywhere. The following are some examples in your personal life:

- House: Rooms: Kitchen, Den, Bedroom, Dining Room, Living Room
- Stores: Type of: Grocery, Book, Sports, Shoe, Music
- Library: Sections: Fiction, Non-Fiction, Historical, Religion, Business

The same model can also be used in your office. Some examples of Support Categories are: Clients, Financial, Policies and Procedures, Literature, Presentations, and Personal.

As humans, we have a tendency to make things complex. God set up our brains to assimilate information by subject. Why fight the simplest and most intuitive way to find something?

In the school of Organization, isn't it time to make Categories your favorite subject?

45

Use the same system to store and access your information.

How many different systems do you use to store information?

You may be using Windows Explorer, a shared drive, e-mail, voice mail, a smartphone, appointment book, file drawer, and on and on and on. Unfortunately, most people use between six to eight different systems for storing information. Many use a different system for each piece of technology. That's reinventing the wheel just a few too many times, isn't it?

By using the same information storage system model everywhere, when you file something or look for something no matter where it is, you'll always be able to find it.

Start counting all the different systems you use. You might be surprised at how many you are using.

Only one is needed.

46

Use the first word that comes to mind when naming a file.

How many times have you been unable to find a file because you forgot what you named it? Search has become your very best friend.

Use the very first word that comes to your mind. If the word "stuff" comes to mind, use stuff. It doesn't matter as long as it's your first word. The harder you try for the correct word, the less chance you'll have of coming up with one that you'll remember.

If I tried to find a soft drink and looked under a file called, "Pop," I'd be looking for a long time unless I was from the Midwest. Coming from Eastern Long Island, I think of the word soda (pronounced so-der). In the South, it's a Coke. In New Orleans, it's a cold drink, and in New Hampshire, it's a tonic.

I wonder what you get when you order a gin and tonic in New Hampshire. Hmm. Make that a water, please.

47

A Form is a Form is a Form is a Form.

Have you ever found that a file can be stored in more than one place?

Think about where to store a form. A form is a template or a blank piece of paper that's not filled out. Potentially you could store a form in a bunch of places (Categories)—Financial, Personnel, or Clients. Basically in any Category that has forms. But where do you store the other forms that don't go into one of the above Categories? Oops! Now you have two or more places to look for forms. Soon to be many more.

When you have trouble knowing where to file something, it's generally because you haven't broken it down into its most basic—pardon the pun—form, i.e., what it really is.

We tend to complicate this process instead of allowing it to be natural, simple and dare say, easy.

The question you want to ask regarding where something goes is: "What is it?" The answer in this case is a Form.

Why not store all of the forms in a place that describes what they really are? A Category called—duh—Forms.

Newsflash: A Book is a Book is a Book is a Book. A book doesn't go into the Financial Category even if it is a financial book. If it has pages and is bound, hopefully for the bookshelf, it's a Book.

Onward to the bookshelf!

48

Your paper, e-mail, and computer file names should all match.

Do you use a different system for storing information in your smartphone, paper, computer, and e-mail files?

If so, a better method is to use the same information storage system everywhere. Start with your computer. Use only one directory in Windows Explorer, such as My Documents, or a shared drive. Create a list of twelve or fewer Support Categories, storing all electronic files under these Categories.

Next, use the same Category names to set up your paper system. (With paper files, assign a color for each Category, such as blue for Forms. A good way to remember the Category color is to tie it into something with which you associate that color, such as "I become depressed and blue when I fill out Forms.")

Use Windows Explorer as the primary place to store your files. In some cases you may want to have both paper and electronic copies. Some examples would be:

    a. You don't want to print out frequently used files, such as forms or brochures, every time you need one so you have a bunch in a hanging folder.

    b. You don't have a scanner or printer to scan in the sheets.

The total number of systems needed is just one.

49

If you listen, you will hear it.

Do you have a hard time coming up with Category names to use for the information you store?

The job of an executive that I was working with was to come up with the name of her Support Categories as we went through each piece of her paper. To say that she was being challenged finding the right names is putting it nicely.

In her hands were articles she had written. I asked her what Category the "articles" should go into. She said she didn't know. I asked again. She said she still didn't know. I kept asking what Category the articles should go into emphasizing the word articles. The tension level was rapidly going past boiling when finally her facial expression softened and she embarrassingly said, "In Articles."

Hmmm. Imagine that. Articles going into a Category called Articles. What will they think of next?

It may seem obvious; but when we are engaged in the battle for the correct Category name, many of us simply don't listen to what that little voice in our head is saying.

Just ask yourself "What is it?" Then wait. When you hear that little voice answer, you've got your Category name.

Or perhaps another type of problem.

50

Create file shortcuts in Windows Explorer.

Have you ever found that a file that you frequently use really needs to be stored in a bunch of different places for different things?

Say it is a New Client form you use with every new customer you work with. It is used when you Coach someone, lead a Workshop, do a Webinar, or make a Speech. You will be using the same form in every case.

Is it really okay to have duplicates in different places? Absolutely. If you update the form, how can you ensure that all of the duplicates will remain the same? Worse, how can you remember where all of the other duplicates are stored in order to make sure you updated all of them?

The answer is by changing the original or root file. When you do, every other shortcut or duplicate file will automatically be changed. Initially, you will always want to locate a file by its subject and by asking "What is it?" If it is a New Client form, you will know to look for it in the Forms Category. Remember, the original root file will answer the question, "What is it? Well, it's a Form." All of the other locations are just dupes or copycats.

Here's how to change it in Window Explorer:

1. Open up Windows Explorer. In Windows 7, right click the Start button on the Task bar and left click on Open Windows Explorer.
2. After Windows Explorer opens, find a file that you want to create a shortcut or duplicate with.
3. Select and right click the file.
4. A drop down menu will appear.
5. Left click on Create shortcut.

A duplicate file will be created right after or below the file you just clicked on in Windows Explorer. The only difference is the new file or duplicate will have a little arrow in the icon preceding the file name and the word Shortcut with it to identify that it is a duplicate. You can now drag that duplicate anywhere you need it such as to Workshops or Speeches. In this case, the root file (and original) will be in Forms.

By the way, who you calling a shortcut?

51

Process your e-mail messages. Don't do them.

Does it seem to take just a little bit longer each time you go through your e-mail? Is it because you are getting more e-mails or perhaps because you were never taught how to go through them?

There is a better way. In fact there is *A Vetter Way*®.

Going through your e-mail Inbox is similar to going through your desk Inbox. You need to make a decision (Process) regarding the e-mail rather than working on (Produce) or doing the e-mail. Processing means deciding, categorizing, prioritizing and dragging the e-mail to the appropriate Action folder—and working on it later. Doing means reading, working on, or replying to it right then.

Why shouldn't you work on them right then? Ironically, because it takes a lot longer when you Process information and Produce work at the same time. Just the opposite of what most of us believe.

Yet another example proving that multitasking (Processing information and Producing work at the same time) isn't productive.

52

Use an Inbox and an Outbox if you use paper.

If you don't have an Outbox, where do you put a piece of paper that you need to give to someone? (Please don't say on your desk or your credenza.)

If you use paper, you need both an Inbox and an Outbox since sometimes you bring paper into your office and other times you take it out. You need a temporary place to hold it.

All paper that comes into your office is always dropped into your Inbox first. If it is in your Inbox, it won't be on your desk, floor or credenza. Process your Inbox contents three times a day, moving it to one of four places: OATS (Outbox, Action, Trash or Support).

Your Inbox is a great place to put anything that is handed to you, or that you bring back to your office from an appointment or a meeting. With no Inbox being used, the paper can be placed on your desk, credenza, or floor—not the best of storage places.

If you have paper, get one.

53

Everything goes into your desk Inbox first.

What do you do with the following?
- Someone hands you a piece of paper.
- You write down a phone number.
- You have papers from a sales appointment you were just on.
- You have a handout from yet another, boring meeting you just attended.

Immediately drop them, dump them, plop them, or, if you're skillful enough, fling them into your Inbox.

By doing this, your desk, floor, walls, and credenza will be paper-free, you'll eliminate having to file the item away right then (you file only when you Process your Inbox three times a day), and, most importantly, you'll be able to finish what you were working on because you won't be distracted with a gazillion things all over your office!

Inbox lamp is lit. Fling 'em if you've got them.

54

From your desk Inbox, there are only four places information can go.

Do you ever pick up a piece of paper in your Inbox and wonder where the silly thing should go? Or do you just kind of leave it alone and never bother it?

During the day, everything always goes into your Inbox first. From there, it goes to one of the following:

- Outbox—Anything that leaves your office or cubicle (or home).
- Action—Anything you intend to work on now or in the future.
- Trash—Anything you no longer use.
- Support—Anything you want to save or refer to, and have no intention of working on.

Everything you keep in your office should either be an Action (something you intend to work on) or a Support (information you save).

Remember your OATS daily, and you'll keep a clean, healthy, and empty Inbox.

55

Deciding rather than Doing is the key to your desk Inbox.

Do you "do" (work on and from) your desk Inbox instead of "deciding" where the contents should go? If so, that may be why it takes so long to go through and empty it (if you do empty it).

There are five steps for going through your desk Inbox:

1. Stand.

   Standing, rather than sitting, allows you to empty your Inbox in less than five minutes.

2. Ask OATS (Outbox, Action, Trash, Support)

   There are only four places an item can go: O—out of your office, A—to work on, T—to throw away or S—to save.

3. Decide the Category and the File

   Once you've decided you need to work on the item (Action) in your Inbox or save the item (Support), you need to identify the Category (the name you will be calling the grouping of similar items) and the File name (what it is) so you can find the item quickly and easily.

4. Use all of your senses

   By using as many senses as you can, you're causing yourself to relearn where the item is stored every time you file it away and every time you look for it. See the item, say what it is, hear yourself say what it is, touch the item, and if you are really weird, smell it.

5. File it

   Put the paper into a hanging folder.

Do not underestimate the power of the Inbox, for in it lays your freedom to make decisions.

56

Stand when you go through your desk Inbox.

How long does it take you to empty your desk Inbox that is if you do at all?

You can empty your Inbox in fewer than five minutes when you stand and use a system versus spending an average of 20-30 minutes when sitting down.

When you sit, your tendency is to want to read or work on what is in your Inbox—exactly what you don't want to be doing then. Your goal is to simply decide and move it to where it needs to go.

The same is true when making phone calls or attending a meeting.

How long do you think meetings would last if everyone was standing?

57

Have an Inbox on one side of your desk and an Outbox on the other.

Is your Inbox on top of your Outbox? If it is, tell it to get off.

The reason many people have an Inbox and Outbox on top of one another is to save desk space. However you won't need to if you only have five items on your desk.

By keeping the boxes on opposite sides of your desk, you are creating a specific energy path or flow of information. "Wax on. Wax off. Paper in. Paper out." Paper flows into your office via your Inbox, goes to you for a decision, and then flows out through your Outbox.

Hey! Could Mr. Miyagi in the Karate Kid movie be wrong?

P.S. Make sure to label your Inbox. Otherwise you have a 50-50 chance of the paper going to the wrong box.

58

Tear off used pages from your legal pads.

How many legal pads do you have with folded over pages?

Folding over pages is a great way to not have to deal with or decide what to do with what is on the pad. It also causes you to use more than one pad at a time, cluttering up your office with multiple pads. ♪ Here a pad, there a pad, everywhere a pad-pad. ♪ Worse, think about all the time you have lost looking back through all those pages when you needed to find something.

When you return to your office, immediately tear off all folded pages on the pad and drop them into your Inbox. Going through your Inbox three times a day will ensure a correct decision as to where the pages need to be filed.

You'll stop flipping out when you stop flipping over your pages.

59

Open your Windows Explorer.

Do you know the difference between Windows Explorer and Internet Explorer? Besides the first word? Many people think they are the same. They aren't close.

Internet Explorer allows you to get onto the Internet. Windows Explorer allows you to find files and folders in seconds by seeing an outline of the programs and folders in your computer. It is kind of like a two dimensional file drawer. It is an ideal place to store information you want to keep and refer to—away from all of your Action stuff.

Here is how to open Windows Explorer in Windows 7:

1. On the bottom of your screen, go to the multicolored circle on the far left side of your Taskbar.
2. Right click the circle.
3. A drop down menu which goes up appears.
4. Left click Open Windows Explorer.
5. Windows Explorer opens up.

Your job is to find one directory to house all of your information in which should be My Documents (or a shared drive if you use one).

In the left window towards the top of the screen, look for an icon that has Desktop next to it. Under that will be a few folders such as Libraries, then under that, Documents, and under that, My Documents.

Double click My Documents. This is where you will be creating your twelve (or fewer) folders (Support Category) and storing your information.

♪ I can see clearly now… ♪

60

Windows Explorer is the quickest and easiest way to find anything.

Are you able to go to just one place on your computer and view all of your files? Most people can't as they are scattered all over.

Store all of your files in one directory in Windows Explorer. That way, when you go to look for a file, they'll all be in one place. If you use My Documents or a shared drive as the directory, when you Save a document, your system can "default" it to a Save As dialogue box with a listing of all your Support Categories. Select the Support Category you want to save the file in and type in the file name. Presto Save-o!

This new way of storing information means that all types of files, such as Word, Excel, and PowerPoint, will be saved under that one particular Category. It's a far cry from the old way of opening Word, selecting Open, and scrolling your life away trying to find that elusive file or having to Search for everything. It's also an easier way to back up your files, since they're all in one directory.

Say "So long" to Scrolling (not to mention Searching) and "Hello" to finding.

61

Save e-mails that you reference to Windows Explorer.

How many folders have you created in your e-mail program to store information in? Probably, more than you would like to admit.

I know it's easier and more convenient to create folders in your e-mail program rather than saving them in Windows Explorer, but there are problems if you do.

1. If it is easy to do, you have a greater chance of doing it.

    Most people's tendency is to save e-mails in Outlook that never should be saved. Why? Because it's so easy to drag the e-mails to a folder in Outlook. When you have to take that extra step to save them in Windows Explorer, you will have to make a good decision as to whether you really need the file or not. By making a better decision, you'll delete e-mails that really need to be deleted.

2. Your Action and Support will be mixed together.

    What happens when you have tasks you need to work on mixed in with reference information you want to save? (Think about your e-mail Inbox or the top of your desk.) You waste a lot of time sorting through stuff. When all of your Action is in one spot, everything you need to work on is right there, broken down for you. All Action goes to Outlook. All Support (Save) goes to Windows Explorer.

3. You will have information in more than one place.

    You will have at least two places on your computer to look for information and maybe more—your e-mail and Windows Explorer. That just adds another place to look, which you really don't want. The goal is to have only one place to look for all of your electronic information storage (Support).

4. It may slow down your server.

    In Outlook, think about the storage space that is needed for everyone saving everything they have had for the past 10 years. Too much data can slow down your server and your retrieval speed. If you think Outlook is slow now, try adding another gigabyte of information for each person. You might want to grab a book while you are waiting, maybe War and Peace.

5. Too many folders.

    How many folders do you have in Outlook? A gazillion? Can you find everything in five seconds? Or is Search your favorite button to push—even more than your younger brother's? Creating folders in Outlook is easy. Unfortunately, the more folders, the longer it takes to find anything. There are only four base Action folders in Outlook and no Support folders. Compare that with the number of folders you have. Uh-oh!

The goal is simple. Have only one place on your computer to look for all of the information (Support) that you save and refer to.

I rest my (brief) case.

62

Drag your Support e-mails to Windows Explorer.

Why would you want to store e-mails you need to work on along with information you just reference? You wouldn't.

Why not simply move, make that drag, all of those non-action e-mails to Windows Explorer so that only actions are in your e-mail.

Here's how in Microsoft Outlook 2013:

1. Open Microsoft Outlook and Windows Explorer.
2. Left click and hold down an e-mail in Outlook that you want to move and save.
3. While holding it down, drag it down and over the Windows Explorer icon that is already open on your Taskbar.
4. Windows Explorer will reopen.
5. Continuing to hold the e-mail down, drag it to and over the Support Category folder you want to store it in.
6. If the folder you want to store it in is a sub folder, hold the e-mail over the folder above the sub folder for a moment. The sub folder will open.
7. Let go.

Dragging and saving your e-mails this way is extremely fast. The only down side is that you keep the original e-mail file name.

Kind of a drag—but not a big one.

63

Leave time open during the day to work.

Do you ever find that your well-planned out day doesn't quite occur the way you want it to?

If your entire day is completely blocked out with appointments and meetings, what happens to your schedule when you run late, an emergency occurs, or you get a last minute e-mail? Worse, when do you actually get any critical work done? (Whatever you do, please do not say after 5 or at home.)

When you set up your day, keep extra time open to get work done (Your Batched, Calendar, Projects, and To Do Categories).

Hint: If everyone has access to your calendar, set up artificial meetings so you can get work done during these times.

Nothing like a mini vacation in the middle of the day!

64

Understand the distinction between Working and Producing.

Do you really get work done when you e-mail someone...or is just information being exchanged?

There is a difference between Working and Producing. Preparing and sending out twenty-five sales proposals is Working. Closing twenty-five sales (or just even one) is Producing.

Working is the act of doing; the motion involved; the effort.

Producing is the accomplishing of a result; the sale that was closed. The product that was made.

Are you working hard but not getting the results you want? When you go through your e-mail, you are definitely Working, but are you really Producing—or are you just moving information back and forth?

It used to be: Work hard.

Then it was: Work smart.

Now it is: Produce a result.

65

Work from a balanced diet of tasks.

What happens when you just eat from one of the food groups such as the Doughnut group? What do you mean there isn't a Doughnut group?

Yeah, yeah, I know. You have heard this before but it also applies to your work life. Many people are primarily working from only one group of tasks: the time-based, reactive, deadline group. Why? They believe they don't have time for anything else. Sometimes you can get away with working that way, but a lot of times you can't.

Every day, work (Produce) from each of your Action Categories:

- Calendar – Tasks that can only be done or must be done on a certain date. Do not put tasks that are due in the future in the Calendar. They go into the To Do.

    Examples: A call to make on a specific date, info to take on a trip, or an appointment on a specific date.

- Batched – Similar types of tasks that can be done together. Think of an assembly line performing the same action.

    Examples: Bills to pay, reports to review, calls to make, e-mails to reply to, articles to read.

- To Do – These are important and impactful tasks that you never seem to have time to do—and many times don't do. Every day, work on your top 5 most important tasks (To Do A's) uninterrupted in your Quiet Time (20% of your work day).

    Examples: Tasks with a due date you can do before they are due, a step of a Project, developing a form or a template that will save you time in the future.

- Projects – These are tasks which are made up of more than one step, you work on with others, or that take a while to get done. Projects can be accomplished one step at a time and by moving or dragging a step to one of the other Action Categories, generally to the To Do A folder to get done.

Examples: The annual conference you are coordinating in Las Vegas, next year's budget, a new software rollout.

Hey! Maybe mom was right about that balanced food thing.

66

Set up your four Action Categories in folders in your e-mail program.

Why would you want your electronic work system to be different from your paper work system?

Today with so much information being electronic, you need to duplicate your paper Action Categories in your e-mail program. The goal is to store all e-mails you need to work on only in your e-mail program and nowhere else on your computer. Your e-mail program becomes (please say it out loud and very military like) "Command Central." This is the one spot that you work from.

Create your four Action Category folders (_Batched, _Calendar, _Projects, and _To Do) under your Inbox folder. The underscore moves them to the top of the list of folders, and above all of the other folders you already have.

- 📁 Inbox
    - 📁 _Batched (similar items)
        - 📁 Call
        - 📁 Data entry
        - 📁 E-mail
        - 📁 Left message
        - 📁 Read
        - 📁 Reply
        - 📁 Sent e-mail
        - 📁 Talk with
            - 📁 Elaine
            - 📁 Jack

Winning the Productivity Game

- 📁 _Calendar (date)
  - 📁 Pending (waiting for something from others without a specific date)
    - 📁 Direct reports (Optional)
      - 📁 Elaine
      - 📁 Jack

(1-31 and Jan-Dec are in your e-mail program calendar)

- 📁 _Projects (a series of steps)
  - 📁 The Project Name (The Guide Sheet with an overview goes here)
    - 📁 Steps (Each separate task to do)
    - 📁 Support (Any non-action information temporarily stored here)
- 📁 _To Do (important tasks)
  - 📁 1-5 (Your top 5 To Do A tasks to work on in your Quiet Time)
  - 📁 A (Very Important) Only your top 5 are moved up to 1-5 daily
  - 📁 B (Important)
  - 📁 C (Somewhat Important)

Once in a while, it is okay have a duplication.

The Department of Redundancy Department.

67

Set up the same four Action Categories in your file drawer as you have in your e-mail system.

Q: Should you use manila folders or hanging folders with your paper system?

A: Hanging folders. In the long run, they are cheaper and don't fall apart. You can also find a tab on a hanging folder much quicker than on a manila folder.

Here are some rules for your Action Category hanging folder system in your file drawer:

- The folders used are letter size hanging folders.

- All folders are always yellow. Why yellow? It's a bright and cheery color. (You can always use the old, drab, military, standard green colored ones if you want. Bah humbug!) Note: Each Support Category will be in a different colored folder other than yellow.
- The following go five tabs across the hanging folder:
  - 1-5
  - 1-31
  - January–December
- A,B,C. Place tab A on far left, tab B in middle, C on far right of hanging folders.
- All others start and go on the far left side, and go from the front to back alphabetically:
- The A, B, and C hanging file folders are stapled shut. They are used as guides only with each To Do task going into a separate hanging folder behind one of them. The empty hanging folders are stored in the front of the drawer right before the To Do #1 hanging folder.

68

Stop with the lists.

Do you use paper To-Do lists?

If so, take the following quiz. Give yourself a point for each one that you use, or have used.

- Assorted commercially produced, multicolored to do list pads.
- Hotel to do list pads.
- Matchbook covers.
- Sugar packets.
- Napkins.
- The back of old notebooks.
- Pages in books.
- Pages in brand new books.
- Pages with no books.

- Pages that have never even seen a book.
- Newspapers. (Never the sports section, please!)
- Legal pads.
- Letter size pads.
- Pizza boxes.
- Back of business cards.
- Index cards.
- Pieces from cardboard boxes.
- Assorted scraps of different sizes of paper.
- Backs of checks.
- Deposit slips.

1–3 You are very Conservation minded. Smokey the Bear would like to meet you.

4–6 You are pretty normal.

7–14 A restraining order to stay away from all paper will soon be sent to you.

15–20 You have just helped the Giant Redwood Trees to become an endangered species.

Do you see a pattern here? In other words, some people think that anything that can be written on or torn off that is handy, can be used as a to-do list.

Perish the thought that one would be organized enough to have the same thing to write on each time such as a 3 x 5 card which is simple, light, easy to carry, fits into a pocket, or appointment book and is mobile.

Choose one…and only one.

♪ Start shredding the lists. I'm leaving tonight. ♪

69

Use a 3 x 5 card to remind yourself of something you need to do.

How many good ideas have you forgotten because you didn't write them down?

When you think of something you want or need to do, immediately write it down on a 3 x 5 card. If you are in the office, drop the card into your Inbox. If you are out, keep the card in your appointment book and then drop it into your Inbox when you get back.

Write down only one action per card. That way, instead of creating a to-do list with tasks that have different characteristics, you will be able to classify them more effectively and file them into the appropriate Action Category:

- Batched—similar types of tasks that can be done together
- Calendar—tasks that can only be done on certain dates or in certain months
- Projects—a big task consisting of a series of small tasks
- To Do—tasks that are important

When the thought hits you, hit back by writing it on a 3 x 5 card no matter what you are doing or where you are.

70

Create an electronic note card reminder in your e-mail program.

Do you have paper notes scattered all over your office?

Welcome to the wonderful world of computers! Instead of using paper, you can create an electronic note card reminder in Microsoft Outlook 2013. Then you can drag your reminder note card into one of your Action Category folders in the left window (Call; E-mail; Read; Talk with) for tasks that you need to do.

Here's how:

1. Select the specific Action Category folder in which you want to file your task (such as in Batched/Call).
2. Click on the Home tab on the Ribbon on top.
3. Click on New Items in the New group.
4. Go down to More Items.
5. Click on Post in This Folder.
6. A page will appear (this is your electronic note reminder that you can use like a paper 3x5 note card but better).

7. Type in the Action you want to take in the Subject line, such as Call Martha.
8. Then click on the Post icon on the top left.

By doing this, you will create a reminder note in the folder you selected in your e-mail program reminding you of a task you need to work on. Electronic note cards allow you to stay paperless and eliminate to-do lists.

These can be used for voice messages eliminating paper lists of people to call back. They can also be saved as a Support information and stored in Windows Explorer, or Forwarded to someone. They are extremely versatile.

♫ Oh where, oh where have my paper notes gone? ♫

71

Think Assembly Line when you work.

Do you run your washing machine for only one item? Of course not! Guys know the correct way is to pack their machine with every piece of clothing they own so it hardly turns. Now that's being productive! Kidding!

Today if you work on tasks as they pop up, you are probably interrupting yourself every two minutes. Think of how many times during the day that you make just one call, or e-mail only one person rather than bunching your calls, or doing your e-mails at the same time.

The Action Category called Batched is a place in your e-mail program that allows you to drag and store similar tasks that can be worked on at the same time. File examples are: Call; Prospects; Read; Talk with; Pay; E-mail; Data entry (Type); Left Message, and Reply.

Running to the copy machine ten times a day is great exercise but doesn't enhance your productivity. Going once or twice does.

How long would a factory stay in business if it didn't use an assembly line?

How long will you stay in business if you don't?

72

Have a file called "Talk With" or "Discuss" in your Batched Category.

Do you ever find that there are certain people with whom you constantly need to talk? What do you do with all those e-mails, scraps of paper, and files with information about which you need to talk with them? (This sounds like a grammar lesson.)

Many people today e-mail someone every time they have a thought. That creates a lot of interruptions— not only for you, but also for them.

Keep the items that you need to talk with them about in a folder or file called Talk With in your Batched Action Category. Talk With provides a place for all those things you want to talk about with your boss, assistant, project manager, or coworker, that you don't know where to keep to remind yourself until you do.

In your hanging folder drawer, right behind Talk With and one tab lane to the right, will be the name of each person you talk with. Drop a 3 x 5 card, a note, or a file into that hanging folder.

In your e-mail program, drag the e-mail that you need to talk with them about to a folder with their name on in the left Folder Pane window. For example it would go under the following: Under your Inbox (folder), under Batched (folder), under Talk with (folder), and under the person's name (folder).

Say good-bye to the assortment of papers, yellow stickies, and e-mails left in your Inbox and forgotten items scattered all over your life and say hello to Talk With.

73

Items that you are waiting for without a specific date go into Pending.

How do you remind yourself of an item you are waiting for that doesn't have a specific due date that you don't want to forget about?

Say you are waiting for the remainder of an important document, but you don't have a specific date for when that final piece will arrive. Where do you keep your document so you can find it easily when the other half arrives?

Some people pick an approximate date they think the document will arrive. Unless you are real lucky, or have a photographic memory, you most likely will have to search through a bunch of dates to find the document, or use Search for the millionth time. Others pick a date that is probably too soon for its arrival, then move the document from date to date to date, handling it countless times until the other half finally arrives.

Instead, simply create a file folder called Pending under your Calendar Action Category. Whenever you are waiting for something that has no specific arrival date, drag (or drop) the item into your Pending folder. Check your Pending folder on Friday when you weekly review your four Action Categories. When the item arrives, you'll know exactly where to find the document you've been holding.

Items with specific dates go into a specific date (1-31 on the Calendar). Dateless items go into Pending (or Singles bars).

74

Sent e-mail is different from Pending

Do items that you are waiting for ever slip through the cracks? How do you keep track of e-mails that you sent to someone that you need a response from?

What do you do when you send an important e-mail to someone and are waiting for a response from them? Drag the e-mail that you sent to a Sent e-mail folder in your Batched Action Category.

The distinction between a Sent e-mail and a Pending is that with a Sent e-mail, you are waiting for a response from someone you e-mailed. The onus is on you regarding the information you requested in the e-mail so you want to make sure they get back with you.

With regard to Pending, you are waiting for a specific item from them after they have acknowledged your e-mail and said they would be sending you something but without a specific date. Drag the e-mail you are waiting for to a Pending folder you have created in the Folder Pane in the left window under the Calendar Action Category folder. If you did have a specific receipt date, you would drag the e-mail to the Calendar icon on that date.

- Sent e-mail — Waiting for a response from someone you sent an e-mail to.
- Pending — Waiting for a specific item from someone who said they would get back with you without specifying a date.

Pending is dateless. Kind of like some of us on a Saturday night. Bah-dah-boom.

75

Stop assigning due dates to every task.

How many times do you assign a due date to a task just to ensure that it gets done?

A due date is an artificial way of causing a task to be accomplished that is one-dimensional. Some due dates are necessary—most aren't. The problem occurs when you consistently slap a due date onto every task. Sadly, it is how most of us have been taught to work.

What happens when you work from this due date mentality? Time rather than importance dictates how you work. "When is it due?"

becomes more important than "How important it is and what its impact is."

How can you expect to successfully drive your organization in the long run if all you're ever thinking about are those annoying due dates?

Many are slapped—few should be.

76

E-mails can go only to one of four places: FADS.

When you open your e-mails, do you just kind of look at them and wonder where they should go? Or do you just leave them in your Inbox and not even consider moving them?

Information from your e-mail Inbox flows to four places the same way as it does from your desk Inbox. All e-mails go to one of the following:

Forward   Forward it. This is the equivalent of using a yellow sticky note on a piece of paper in your Outbox. Limit it to one sentence, please.

Action   Drag the e-mail to one of your Action Category folders in your e-mail program. Or print out the Action and place it into your desk Inbox.

Delete   Delete it.

Support   Save it in a Support Category folder in Windows Explorer.

Remember, if you look at it, move it.

77

Completely empty your e-mail Inbox.

How many e-mails do you have left in your Inbox when you are done going through it? If the answer is anything other than zero, the next question is "How come?"

Many people work from and out of their e-mail Inbox—the same way they go through their desk Inbox, which is a Bozo no-no.

When you leave an e-mail in your Inbox, that e-mail and all the other e-mails that you didn't do anything with, other than just look at, will still be sitting there the very next time you check your e-mail. Every time you look at an e-mail you have already looked at is time you are throwing away. Not only that, but after a while, all those critters will start adding up, causing you to have an awful lot of e-mails you have to look through—again and again.

The answer is to make a decision and move each e-mail. There are only four places e-mails can go: FADS (Forward, Action, Delete, Support)

Remember, this time, having none is good!

78

E-mails to call on a date can be dragged to the Calendar.

Here is how to remind yourself to make a call on a specific date by only using the e-mail.

1. Select the e-mail message in Outlook of the person you need to make a call to on a specific date.
2. Drag it to the date in the To-Do Bar on the right or down to the Calendar icon (depends on your version of Outlook).
3. A dialogue box will appear.
4. Make sure the Appointment tab is selected at the top of the dialogue box.
5. Click on the drop-down arrow on the Start time box and select the date you need to make the call.
6. Check off the All day event box. This will place the e-mail call reminder at the very top of the selected date page and not on a specific appointment time in your Day Calendar view.
7. Click on the Save & Close button on the top left.

Winning the Productivity Game

This allows you to keep the e-mail in the system without having to print it out or leave it in your Inbox to be reminded to do it.

Freedom!

79

You can save an e-mail with its attachments to a specific date.

Where do you keep an e-mail you need for a specific meeting? Don't you dare say your Inbox.

You can keep an e-mail with attachments you need for an appointment in your Outlook 2013 Calendar. However, if you try to drag it to the Calendar icon, you'll lose the attachment. Here's how not to lose the attachment:

1. Select the e-mail.
2. Click on the Home tab on the Ribbon on the top.
3. Next click on the Move icon in the Move group. A drop down list will appear.
4. Click on Other folders.
5. Click on Calendar.
6. An appointment screen will appear.
7. Set the date by clicking on the Start time date down arrow.
8. A mini-calendar will appear. Click on the desired date.
9. For a specific appointment time, click on the Time down arrow.
10. Select Save and Close.

The e-mail will appear at your appointment time on that date when you click the Day button on the Ribbon in your Calendar. You can open the e-mail and review its contents and attachments for your meeting by simply clicking on it.

You look so much smarter when you have all of the facts!

80

Tasks which are too big to do can be made into Projects.

What is a Project anyway (besides something you never want to do)?

A Project is simply a large task that you can't get done at one sitting. This is especially true if you work with others and get to go to those fun meetings and endlessly discuss irrelevant topics. Projects that can be done at one sitting are called To Do's. You are able to get To Do's done because they are smaller and quicker than Projects.

A Project is made up of a Guide Sheet and a bunch of Step sheets. The Guide Sheet gives you an overall view of what needs to be done; it is where you work from. A Guide Sheet will have a numbered list of all of the tasks (Steps) you need to do to complete the Project.

You need to create a Step sheet for every Step on your Guide Sheet. Each Step sheet is what enables you to work on only one Step at a time. When you are done with a Step, check it off of the Guide Sheet, and then work on the next Step. Eventually you will get all of the Steps done.

Many years ago when I was a Social worker, the following was sent in: "My husband recently had his project cutoff and I haven't had any relief since."

Whatever you do, don't allow your Project to get cut off. If you work on only one Step at a time, I can guarantee it won't.

81

Break your Projects into small pieces.

Have you ever started to work on a Project the day you received it? Neither have I. Working on Projects is right up there with going to the dentist and doing your taxes.

Think about how you cheat on a diet. Take a piece of cake for instance, which obviously wouldn't be on your diet. You just pick off a little piece, justifying that it really won't count since it is, after all, so small and not a real piece. Then another small piece and another and another. "Hey, I'm not really eating it. I'm just having a little piece here and there." Before you know it, the cake is gone.

You can use that same wonderful skill you've developed through the years of cheating on your diet to make working on Projects easier. Just like those pieces of cake that mysteriously vanished due to the cultivated art of being a skillful picker, so can your Projects vanish—piece by small piece.

Make the steps to a Project as small as possible and then let them eat cake.

82

80% of getting a Project done is setting up the Guide Sheet.

Do you have a hard time finishing a Project? Or worse, starting one? Are all Project related e-mails unmercifully crammed into one big folder with no Project guide in sight? Sounds about right.

Getting a Project done quicker and easier is about setting up that darn Guide Sheet that you never seem to be able to do. A Guide Sheet gives you a complete overview of a Project with milestones and a list of all of the steps that you can think of at the time of set up. (You will add a bunch more Steps as you go.)

You can create a Guide Sheet as an Excel document then drag it to Outlook to the folder name of the Project. Clicking on the Excel Guide Sheet form when in the Right Reading Pane view allows you to see the form in the right window and what step you are on. Instant overall Project awareness!

Imagine having a preset list of short and easy tasks to do so you don't have to waste time trying to figure out what you need to do next. Instead of all that thinking about what is next to do, you just do the next well thought out step.

Whatever is this world coming to? Hopefully a lot more Guide Sheets.

83

Filling out the Guide Sheet is the key to accomplishing a Project.

Q: What is the hardest part of getting a Project done?

A: Starting it.

Many people have a hard time starting a Project and procrastinate on them. Some never even do them. Getting the Guide Sheet filled out and set up is the key to getting a Project started and done quickly. After the Guide Sheet is set up, working on the Project is easy since now you are just basically working on a bunch of small and easy to do tasks (Steps).

You can create a Guide Sheet form in Microsoft Word or Excel that you can use for each Project. Drag the Guide Sheet form (that you keep in Windows Explorer under the Forms Support Category) to the folder of the Project name in your e-mail program.

- 📁 Inbox
    - 📁 _Projects
        - 📁 The Project name. (The Guide Sheet is dragged here.)
            - 📁 Steps (This is where you keep the Steps of the Project.)
            - 📁 Support (Upon Project completion, files from here can be saved to Windows Explorer or deleted.)

In Outlook, using the Right Reading Pane view allows you to easily see the Guide Sheet and the Step you are currently on in the right window. You must, however, open the Guide Sheet to make any changes to it such as when you are checking off a completed Step.

For a Step, you can use an existing e-mail, a New Post in This Folder card in Outlook, or any other document (Word or Excel). Steps of a Project are dragged from the Project/Steps folder to one of the other three Action Categories—usually the To Do A folder, to be done.

GUIDE SHEET EXAMPLE

PROJECT: _____   TARGET DATE: _____

DUE DATE	DONE	STEP
__ / __ / __	☐	1. _____
__ / __ / __	☐	2. _____
__ / __ / __	☐	3. _____
__ / __ / __	☐	4. _____
__ / __ / __	☐	5. _____

84

He who originates it, keeps it.

How many times during the day do you wonder if you should keep something that someone has e-mailed to you?

An easy way to decide who should keep the e-mail is to follow the "Origination Rule" which states that the person who originates it, keeps it. (This unbeknown to most people, has been passed down for thousands of years.)

This works extremely well unless you work for someone. Then "The Golden Rule" applies. They have the gold so they get to tell you what to do and what to keep (usually everything).

Darn. Guess it's time to get a promotion.

85

Brevity communicates.

Have you ever received a directive, an e-mail, or a voice mail that went on and on and on to the point that you wanted to scream at the top of your lungs in utter frustration since you absolutely had no idea what the person was asking for or trying to tell you and there was so much content in the communication that you felt that you absolutely had to read it all for fear of missing something and if you did miss something that you would get into trouble if you were supposed to do something and you didn't and are you feeling that same feeling right now reading this ridiculously long sentence?

Being brief and to the point works wonders…in the giving and especially in the receiving of information. People get brief…and if not, can always ask for more.

Brief(s) or boxers? Which will it be?

86

Bite your tongue.

Have you ever spoken to a group when you noticed your mouth getting really dry? And you started to panic wondering whether you had enough saliva to spit out another word? Suffering Succotash!

The next time you do, just bite your tongue. That's right. Bite your tongue, but ever so gently.

By biting your tongue, your mouth will become instantly moist allowing you to continue dazzling your audience with your words of wisdom, or with whatever it is that you are ranting about at the time.

My old girlfriend Martha told me this was the trick she used on stage when singing. So either singing or speaking, no more dry mouth.

Remember: Bite me.

87

Send a written Thank You note.

When was the last time you received a written Thank You note? Can you even remember the last one you received?

Now, instead of receiving Christmas cards I sometimes get Christmas e-mails. Yikes!

This may not appear to be a productive use of your time since it takes more time to write a card than to send an e-mail, but in the long run, it pays big dividends.

If you want to be remembered, start writing.

88

Use a five step approach to speaking

Why do you enjoy listening to some speakers while others put you into a Dumbo Doze? Could it be because they know a secret that the others don't?

The next time you find yourself in front of a crowd, at least one that you are speaking to, use the following 5 steps:

1. Hook them.

    Get them interested in what you are saying by asking questions that they want or need an answer to. You will grab the majority of the audience's attention by asking three different questions. They will actually want to hear your solutions now that you have teased them.

2. Give them a consequence for not taking an action.

    After you have their attention, alert them to what will happen if they don't do what you said. Basic cause and effect stuff that they need to be reminded of. For example, "If you don't exercise, your blood will solidify in your body and then explode." Nothing like adding a motivational element to really perk up your audience's interest.

3. Tell them what they are going to learn.

   Many people learn best by understanding the big picture—rather than with pieces of disjointed information randomly flung at them. Outline your points so they can understand the exciting adventure you are about to take them on. "Tonight, you will learn these three amazing things..."

4. Tell them how to do it.

   This is the nuts and bolts part. Unfortunately for many speakers, this is their entire speech. A big how-to do something. Not much of a set up to get the audience interested and excited about what will be said. Yawn!

5. Tell them what you just told them and call them to action.

   Some of us are having trouble with our short term memory so nothing like an update of what was just said 30 minutes ago. After summarizing the points you just gave them, give them a simple action that will get them up and running to solve their problem.

Some of us are having trouble with our short term memories so nothing like an update of what was just written a sentence ago.

Was I supposed to get up and run?

89

Call people who like to listen. E-mail or text people who like to read.

Are your e-mails or phone calls being returned?

If not, you might want to think about enrolling in the Dale Carnegie course, "How to Win Friends and Get People to Call You Back." If they still aren't after that, you might want to change how you are communicating with them.

Winning the Productivity Game

Some people enjoy reading while others enjoy hearing. Actually it goes beyond enjoyment. It has to do with how people process information—some best while reading, others while hearing.

Finding out how others process information will help you get your message across.

The question to ask is "How important is it that the recipients get what you are saying?"

How they receive information matters. Not how you like to send it.

Different strokes for different folks.

90

Cut down on clicks by making it a Favorite.

When you want to save a document or an e-mail to a shared drive, isn't it a pain to have to endlessly click, click and click in the Save As box until you find the drive?

No more.

Here is a way to cut down the clicks.

1. Open Microsoft Windows Explorer by right clicking the Start button on the far left of your Taskbar.
2. Left click on "Open Windows Explorer" which will open up Windows Explorer.
3. Select (or left click one time) the drive/folder that you want to have available.
4. Go to the top left and right click the word "Favorites."
5. Click on "Add current location to Favorites."

From now on your group can save all of their documents to one drive with minimal clicks giving everyone access to all files.

A little click will do ya.

91

Brush up your formatting with the Format Painter.

Does trying to format a Word document really confuse you? It did me until my computer consultant taught me a simple trick.

Say you have a Word document that you are working on and you want to use the same font, letter size, indentations etc. (format) on a section that you used at the beginning of the document. In the middle section of the document, you changed the format. Now at the end of the document you want to use that same beginning format. How can you?

Here's how:

1. Open the existing Microsoft Word 2013 document you want to change.
2. Select the area of the document whose format you want to use on the current section.
3. After selecting it, go to the Ribbon on the top of the page and click on the Home tab.
4. Under the Home tab, go to the Clipboard group and click on the Format Painter (the paintbrush) icon.
5. Next, select the new area whose format you want to change.
6. Release your finger on the mouse.

Your new section will be formatted the same as the beginning section.

That one simple formatting step has paid for the cost of my computer consultant many times over.

Pick up that brush and take a swipe at saving time.

92

Underscore the files you want to save.

How often do you go through your computer files and completely clean them out? I know, next question.

Years ago, while working at a company, a non-training participant whisked me over to his desk to brag about its cleanliness. Curious as to his motivation, I asked if I could take a look in his desk drawer. As I went to open one, a scream of "Nooooooooooo" could be heard three floors above and below us. I guess he didn't want me to look.

Messy desks no longer seem to be the rage. After all, you can only stack so much paper on your desk before it will topple over. No such problem with the computer though. You can pack that baby with everything you own, maxing out every byte of memory. And the best part? No one ever knows your little secret.

From now on, use an underscore on files you want to save. Every time you open a file (and want to save it) in one of your Support Categories in Windows Explorer/My Documents, put an underscore in front of it such as _Phone expenses. That way, you will know which files you have looked at and decided to save. Additionally, using an underscore will move those files to the top of the page making them easier to find.

Eventually you will have underscored files on the top and files on the bottom that you haven't looked at in a very long time. Guess what you get to do with the ones on the bottom?

Here's to a clean desk, make that, a clean computer, in the New Year!

93

A version control.

When revising a document, do you ever get confused as to which is the most recent of the zillion versions that you now seem to have? Are you finding countless clones with slight file name variations?

There is a simple solution. Drag the document from Windows Explorer (Support), to Outlook (Action), make the changes, and then drag the document back to Windows Explorer.

Store documents you refer to (Support) in a Category in Windows Explorer. Keep tasks to work on or to make changes to (Action) in a folder in Outlook.

When you need to revise a document, with Outlook and Windows Explorer open (their icons will appear on the Taskbar on the bottom), left click the document in Windows Explorer, and drag it down to the Outlook icon on the Taskbar. As you do, say "Open sesame!" Outlook will magically open. Continue holding down and dragging the document to an Action folder in Outlook. Then release it.

After you have made the changes to the document, left click it and drag it down to the Windows Explorer icon on the Taskbar. Again, magically Windows Explorer opens (but only if you say "Open sesame!"). Continue holding down and dragging it to the Support Category folder it goes into. Then release it.

But wait. It won't let you save it because the document has been changed. A "Confirm File Replace" dialogue box will ask you if you want to save the changes you made to it.

If you only want one version—the latest and greatest version, with the most recent changes on it—click Yes.

If not, you can save it somewhere else by renaming this new version.

Try to control your versions, would you?

94

Back up right now on paper.

Have you ever been burglarized and lost everything? No computer, phone, fax, or TV? Talk about feeling disconnected...

If you have, how do you get yourself back up and going?

A secret decoder ring? Maybe back in the fifties but not today. Just a simple sheet of paper with the following phone numbers on it will do it:

Phone numbers needed:

- Police. Don't touch anything so they can check for fingerprints.
- Insurance company. Call them right after you call the Police.
- Computer store. So you can purchase a new computer.
- Computer tech. To help you set up your new computer, etc.
- Carpenter. In case your front door is smashed in and you want to secure your house. It's nice to have a front door at night when you are in bed. It gives you kind of a warm, secure feeling.
- Back up cloud storage company. The best money you will ever spend for your business. If you don't have a cloud service, stop what you are doing right now and get one. Hard drives can be stolen along with everything else you own. Carbonite or iDrive are two good ones.

Other ideas

- Have a record. Take a movie of everything in your house. You'd be amazed at the number of things which were stolen that you will forget about until you need them.
- Passwords. Do not keep them on your computer. Keep them on a sheet of paper hidden away.
- Computer. Set up a Password or a fingerprint scan to be able to use your computer. Otherwise the information on your computer is an open book.
- Serial numbers. Keep them on a sheet of paper hidden away for the police and insurance company.
- A chip. Attach a chip to everything you can. Please refrain from doing this with your dog.

Losing information on your computer is like concrete cracking. It isn't whether the concrete is going to crack, it's when and where it will crack. That's why they put joints in every 8-10 feet. To control the cracks.

Likewise, it isn't a matter of IF you'll lose your data, it's WHEN you'll lose it.

Save it on a piece of paper? Really? Yup.

95

Highlight the words that you need to work on.

How can you remind yourself which part of a document you need to change or work on in the future?

The answer: Highlight the words with a bright color. Here's how in Microsoft Word 2013:

1. Open a Microsoft Word document.
2. On the Ribbon on top, click on the Home tab.
3. Look for the Font Group under it.
4. Go to the Text Highlight Color icon (it has an ab with a marker as its icon). Left click the drop down arrow to the right and choose the color for your selected text
5. When you click on the arrow icon, a palate of colors will appear.
6. Click on a color you like (such as sunshiny yellow).
7. You are ready to highlight. Find the words on the document that you want to remind yourself to work on in the future.
8. Left click the word or group of words and select them.
9. With the words selected, click on the Text Highlight color icon.

Suddenly the words explode with a bright burst of yellow.

The next time you are hit with burst of color while reading that document, there will be no doubt as to what needs to be worked on.

Spring has sprung!

96

Save only the attachments from an e-mail.

You have the choice of saving one attachment or as many of the attachments as you want from an e-mail. Here's how in Microsoft Outlook 2013.

1. Select or click on the e-mail.

2. Click on the File tab on the Ribbon on the top of your screen.
3. Select Save Attachments.
4. A Save All Attachments dialogue box will open. All of the attachments will be highlighted.
5. If you are saving all of them, click the OK button. If you are just saving one of them, left click on the attachment you want to save (it will stay highlighted). Click the OK button.
6. A Save Attachments dialog box will appear.
7. In the long horizontal address bar on the top, click on Documents. Your Support Categories will appear.
8. Double click on the Category you want to save the attachment in.
9. Click the OK button.

Don't get too attached to them now that they are easy to save.

97

Delegate rather than work late.

How many tasks are you doing that one of your employees could be working on instead?

Rule of Delegation: It is better to give…to someone…than to do it yourself.

In fact, delegate everything you can and then follow up. Better yet, delegate the follow up to your Assistant or Admin. Your employees were hired to perform specific jobs—let them. Get out of their way. Their performance won't always be perfect, no doubt about that, but it will allow you to focus on that one thing that you are supposed to be doing that you are not doing since you are doing that thing that they could be doing. Whew!

Hey, just delegate it, would you?

P.S. Remember that old disco tune by Three Dog Night? ♪Celebrate! Celebrate! Dance to the music.♪

That's what you'll be able to start doing on Friday nights when you start to Delegate instead of working late.

98

Keep only five things on your desk.

Be honest. How many items do you have on your desk?

The following should be the only five things on your desk other than the task on which you are working. Everything else should be in a drawer, on a shelf, or in your computer.

1. Inbox. (On one side of your desk. If you have any paper, you need one.)
2. Outbox. (On the other side of your desk, not on top of your Inbox. Ditto!)
3. Desk Phone. (On the opposite side of the hand you write with.)
4. Computer. (Best if the keyboard can slide out from under the middle of your desk.)
5. Smartphone, calculator or appointment book. (Whichever you use.)

Next time, instead of dropping an item on your desk, drop the item into your Inbox.

A clean desk is a happy desk!

99

Every loose paper on your desk is a decision not made.

Why do you think your desk and office are so cluttered? Hint: It's not because the cleaning lady didn't come.

Every time you put a piece of paper down, in effect you are choosing not to make a decision about that piece of paper. Why? Perhaps because the decision is too uncomfortable or too painful to make.

The next time you feel the urge to lay down a piece of paper, take a deep breath and become conscious of what you are about to do. Heck it's okay if you put the paper down and don't make a decision. What matters is that you become aware of the process—and what happens to your life when you don't make decisions.

Change occurs only after awareness.

100

The less you have on your desk, the less you will be interrupted.

Is your desk blanketed with paper?

Imagine a video camera recording your head movement as you scan your paper covered desk. You'd probably see your head twisting and turning faster than Linda Blair's did in The Exorcist.

Many people who complain about being interrupted have cluttered desks. Yet if you ask them the source of their interruptions, few would say their desk. Every scrap of paper has the potential to interrupt them—and generally does.

If it's right there in front of you, you will look at it. If you look, you will be interrupted.

Guar-roon-teed!

101

Create boundaries in your life.

How many items do you have on your desk? On your floor?

Being cluttered and feeling overwhelmed is generally not about paper or organization but rather about how well you establish boundaries in your life.

The more boundaries you create and honor, such as limiting your work hours, taking a Quiet Time every day, working only on week days, or having five items on your desk, the more you will feel in control.

Now please make room for that poor car that won't fit into your garage. He's cold and he wants back in.

102

Make a decision with every item on your desk.

What do you do when you pick up something on your desk and don't know what to do with it?

You place it on:

- Your credenza.
- A pile on your desk.
- A spot on the floor—but off to the side, of course.
- Under your desk where no one can see it.
- All of the above.
- None of the above. You just stand there with it in your hand, frozen like a deer in a car's headlights.

The next time you mindlessly plop down a piece of paper, stop, take a deep breath, and make a decision as to where it goes. You'll be amazed at how clean your desk will stay by making a simple decision—and how focused your mind will be.

Warning: Making decisions can be painful, especially when you are not in the habit of making them. But boy, it sure feels good after you do—and your office doesn't look too shabby either.

103

Keep your smartphone on the same spot on your desk.

Do you ever forget where you left your smartphone? Excuse me. More importantly, where you left the remote?

Imagine if your smartphone was connected by a wire to a specific location in your house—just the way phones used to be. Now pick two or three places that you will keep it.

When you put your smartphone down you will be "mentally connected" to store it in those two or three places—always knowing where it will be when you need it.

By the way, where is that remote? The game is on.

104

Ten things you should never, ever do with e-mail.

Be honest. Are you really using e-mail as productively as you could?

Few people have ever been taught a good e-mail system despite the fact that they will receive over a gazillion or so e-mails in their lifetime. Many people use the same system to handle e-mail as they did to handle paper.

How many of these do you do?

1. Open an e-mail, read it, and then leave it.
2. Don't completely empty your e-mail Inbox.
3. Use e-mails in your Inbox as a place to remind you of what to work on.
4. Constantly scroll up and down on your list of Inbox e-mails so you don't forget to do something.
5. Continuously check your e-mail (average device checking today is 150 times per day).
6. Constantly use Search to find something.
7. Immediately reply to the e-mail when you first open it. (The "Only touch a piece of paper once" incorrect belief.)
8. Have your e-mails interrupt you upon their arrival.
9. Keep e-mails that you need to work on (Action) with e-mails that you are saving (Support).
10. Use the Off View (e-mails lined up in a list) when viewing e-mails in your Inbox. Worse, have your Message or Auto Preview on at the same time! (Yikes!!!)

How you scored:

0	You may have a future in the Productivity business.
1–3	Pretty good.
4–5	Trouble is a' brewing.
6–9	Time to get down and dirty and make some big changes.
10	Call me as soon as you can.

105

Free e-mails that are being blocked.

Can anyone ever really want another e-mail sent to them?

Once in a while, you may want to receive a specific e-mail from someone that your Junk E-mail is preventing you from receiving.

Here is how you can add that e-mail to your Safe Sender's list.

1. In Outlook 2013, click on the Home tab on the Ribbon on top.
2. Go to the Delete group area.
3. Go to Junk.
4. Click on the arrow to the right of Junk.
5. Click on Never Block Sender.

Free Willy…then free your e-mails.

106

Change the heading names on your Sort by bar in Outlook.

Do you ever want to change the headings on your Sort by bar in the right window of Outlook? Now you can.

1. Open up the Bottom Reading Pane window.
2. Select the (Action) folder you want to change in the Left Folder Pane window—say the Sent e-mail folder that you created in order to keep track of certain e-mails that you sent out.
3. Right click on the Sort by: bar which is along the top of the right window. (It should already contain various headings such as: From, Subject, Received, Size, etc.)
4. A drop down box will appear.
5. Scroll down and click on Field Chooser.
6. A Field Chooser dialogue box will appear. Pick out the headings that you want for each folder. The headings you choose will vary depending on which you need for each of the (Action) folders that you have selected.

Winning the Productivity Game

7. Drag and drop the headings from the Field Chooser box to the spot along the Sort By bar where you want the new heading to be located.

For example, if you had picked "To" to add to it, when you select the Sent E-mail folder in the Left Folder Pane window, you will now have "To" located on the far left of the Sort by bar followed by the other headings you have chosen.

This sort of works fairly well.

107

Answer with a repetitive e-mail response.

How many times do you reply to an e-mail using the same response? When someone asks, "How are you?" you might typically answer, "Fine thanks. And you?" Imagine if you could train your e-mail to respond to FAQs using the same answer.

Eureka! You can. Here's how.

1. Open Microsoft Outlook 2013.
2. Open an e-mail message.
3. Click on the Message tab on the Ribbon on the top.
4. In the Respond Group, click on the Reply icon.
5. Next click on the Signature icon. A drop down box will appear.
6. Click on Signatures.
7. A Signatures and Stationery dialogue box will appear.
8. Click on the e-mail Signature tab.
9. This is where you get to create and type your response.
10. Click on the New button. A dialogue box will appear.
11. Type in the name you want to call your response such as "Unsubscribe."
12. Now go to the open box on the bottom and type in your message such as "For the hundredth time, would you please unsubscribe me from your e-mails? Have a nice day."
13. Click the OK button.

Now, when you want to unsubscribe from receiving an e-mail:

1. Open the e-mail.
2. Click on Reply.
3. Go to Signatures, click on it
4. When a drop down menu appears, click on Unsubscribe.
5. Click on Send.

Presto. Instant un-subscription.

108

Change e-mail attachments that were sent to you.

Has anyone ever sent you an e-mail attachment that they wanted you to review, make a change to and then send back but it wouldn't let you save the changes on the e-mail? Whatever were they thinking about at Microsoft that day?

Here's how to in Microsoft Outlook 2013

1. Open the e-mail.
2. On the Ribbon on top, click on the Message tab.
3. Look for the Move group of icons under it.
4. Click on the Actions icon.
5. Click on Edit message.
6. Open the attachment.
7. Type in your changes.
8. Hit the Save button.
9. Exit out.

Change is good (as long as it's someone else who's doing the changing).

109

Rename your e-mail messages when you save them.

Do you save your e-mails using the same file name that they came to you with? How can you expect to find them if someone else has named them?

Winning the Productivity Game

When you save an e-mail message or attachment, rename it with a word that comes to your mind—not someone else's.

Don't even get me started with saving them as numbers.

There is no easier way to find something than by using your very own words.

110

Use a different e-mail template for your coworkers.

Would you really want to start off an e-mail to a potential customer with the following at the top of the page?

I need you to do this:

Probably not if you want to keep their business. You may, however, want to use it with your employees so they would know exactly what you needed them to do.

In Microsoft Outlook 2013, you can use different e-mail templates depending on the situation. Here's how to use a different e-mail template that you created:

1. Open Outlook 2013.
2. On the Ribbon on the top, click on the Home tab.
3. Go to the New group.
4. Click on the New Items icon. A drop down menu will magically appear.
5. Click on E-mail Message Using.
6. The various e-mail templates that you created (by changing your Signature) will appear on the right.
7. Click on the desired template named, say, Co-workers.

Viola! The next time you want to send an e-mail to anyone else, click on the New E-Mail Message icon that you normally would do when sending an e-mail and your old e-mail template will magically appear.

As Roy Rogers and Dale Evans would sing: ♪Happy e-mails to you, until we tweet again.♪

111

What goes around comes around.

When you were making a list of what you wanted for Christmas last year, did you by any chance ask Santa for more e-mails?

Of course you didn't. If you asked for anything (other than the Porsche), it would have been for fewer e-mails, not more.

Why would you ever expect to receive fewer when you send out more and more every day? (Note: This is where you blame other employees and your mean boss for sending the e-mails. It is called Denial.)

Here are a few solutions for cutting down the number of companywide e-mails:

- Reply All.

Think before using the Reply All button (or as I call it, the Button of doom).

Three people sending 3 e-mails to one another, and then Replying to All of them, and then Replying to All of them again, means 54 e-mails being created and circulated among 3 people.

- Combine.

No, not the farm machine, bunch them together. Rather than answering every e-mail one at a time, think about combining answers using one e-mail.

- Talk with

You can store e-mails to answer in a folder called Talk with or Discuss in your e-mail program under the Batched Action Category.

- Call.

Calling allows you to come to a conclusion and decision much faster than e-mail ever will—especially with complex issues.

- Ask out.

Let the sender know in a polite way when you don't want to be copied. Many workers aren't sure if you want the information or not so they send it. This is your chance to let them know that you absolutely, positively, definitely, do not want to receive it.

Someone has to stop this insanity.

If you send it, it will come back again, and again, and again.

112

There are basically two reasons for using e-mail.

How can you abuse e-mail? Let me count the ways.

Sending jokes, copying everyone in the known universe, playing e-mail tag, and e-mailing rather than calling are just a few.

The following are the main reasons to send an e-mail:

1. Sending documents and files.

    Probably the greatest benefit of e-mail is being able to send a file or document instantly to someone. It's the Post Office without the attitude, lines, cost, and wait. Have you ever heard of a computer "going postal"?

2. Efficiently sending information to a large number of people.

    Obviously, e-mail allows you to notify a large group of people very efficiently. However when you hit the Reply to All or "Button of Doom," as I call it, you are treading on dangerous ground. It gives new meaning to the terms "information overload," "CYA," and "information bytes" (it sure does). Strings of seemingly never-ending e-mails continually circulate throughout a company's network, many never to be answered.

Sometimes it is better to let your fingers do the walking—to your phone.

113

Have the Ribbon area always visible on top.

When sending an e-mail in Outlook 2013, do you ever find that when you want to make a last minute change to your Word attachment, the Word document opens up (in the Reading view) with the Ribbon area on top hidden so you can't edit the attachment? Bummer!

Well hide me no more. Here is how to always keep that puppy visible on top.

1. Open up Microsoft Word 2013.
2. Click on the File tab on the Ribbon on the top left.
3. Click on Options.
4. A Word Options dialogue box opens up.
5. Click on General.
6. Go to Start Up Options.
7. Uncheck the box in front of: Open e-mail attachments.

From now on, the Ribbon and all of its icons will be visible for your editing pleasure.

Go ahead. Make my change…a last minute change.

114

Know when to call and when to e-mail.

Do you ever feel as if people are e-mailing you when what they should be doing is calling?

Let's face it. E-mail has gotten out of control almost as much as the IRS has. Well, maybe not that much but close. Used incorrectly, e-mail can cause a long, series of time-consuming, never-ending strings and threads of information, with both you and the recipient not having a clue as to what is being asked or stated. Sometimes the issue is too complicated to be communicated through an e-mail. Many times talking to someone is quicker and more efficient.

E-mail is also a great way to skirt the issue, CYA, not be present with, be less responsible, and shift the onus of action onto the other person.

To e-mail or to call. That is the question.

115

Limit your Cc's.

Can you imagine the number of Cc e-mails that are being sent daily? "Billions and billions" as Carl Sagan would say.

Before e-mail, it was estimated that a single document in a company was copied 19 times. Today, with the ability to send more Cc's than stars in the skies, you may soon be hearing: "Houston, we have a problem."

Why are so many copies being sent? Do you really need to be copied on every item? Or are Cc's just a bad habit you developed along with everyone else? You know…to cover yourself…just in case something happens.

The next time you get the urge to send a copy, pinch yourself—rather strongly. That's the pain the other person will feel when he or she is forced to read yet another Cc.

Do a good turn. Stop Cc'ing everybody. Believe me, they will be grateful and so will the universe…with one less Cc to read. Gazillions of hours are being wasted just from opening, reading, shuffling, and storing unnecessary Cc's.

Make that billion and billions.

116

Reply with "Do I really need this?

How many Cc'ed e-mails do you receive that you shouldn't? What do you do about them other than grumble and delete them (or worse, leave them in your Inbox)?

Greg Vetter

You would never want to hurt someone's feelings and tell them you didn't need the e-mail, would you? Maybe it's time to do something.

Take the back of your right hand, put it on your forehead and say, "Poor me! What can I do? There are just too many of them." Then, when you are done playing victim, send a "Do I really need this?" reply. That should stir up the pot some.

Why are they sent?

- Some people feel as if they are helping you.
- A lot believe that they are supposed to be sending them.
- A few are just lazy.
- A bunch are playing CYA.
- Many are overwhelmed and just don't think about it.

None of the above reasons matter. You will still receive the dopey things, and lose valuable time until you say no.

Go ahead. Make their day...with a reply.

117

Standardize an e-mail template.

Don't you just love to receive lengthy e-mails only to have absolutely no idea what you are supposed to do with them?

By standardizing your group's or company's e-mail template, you no longer have to play Sherlock Holmes trying to figure out what someone wants you to do. By listing "What I need from you or Please do this" at the beginning or top of the e-mail, the reader will instantly know what action they need to take.

Plus, you don't even have to open the message if your Bottom Reading Pane is open and the horizontal split bar is almost at the top. Doing it this way allows you to scan the top part of the e-mail message.

Example:

> Please do this:
>
> Regarding:
>
> The format I need it in (e-mail, paper, call):
>
> Priority (A, B, C):
>
> Due date: __ / __ / __

Elementary, my newly organized Watson.

118

Put an A or an S in the e-mail Subject line when someone is traveling.

You're on the road again...perhaps with Willie. As if your daily routine wasn't messed up enough, you also have a gazillion e-mails to go through when you are in an unfamiliar territory. How can you possibly read and do something with all of them?

The next time you are on the road for the week, ask your staff to do this. Type an A or S at the beginning of the Subject line of their e-mails to you. By them typing an A (for Action), you will be alerted that you need to do something with the e-mail.

By them typing an S (for Support) you will know that the information doesn't require an action. It can be saved in Windows Explorer without needing to be read or any action taken.

That way, you can spend your valuable time on important things such as fighting traffic to the airport, waiting in line to be frisked, and then trying to find your hotel room, if they even reserved it for you.

There's no place like home.

119

Take a stroll rather than a scroll.

(Sung to the tune of the TV show *Rawhide*, also featured in *The Blues Brothers* movie.)

♪Scrolling. Scrolling. Scrolling. Keep them e-mails going. Gee my fingers swollen. Rawfingers.♪

Three questions:

1. Do you store e-mails in your Inbox?
2. Do you work from your Inbox?
3. Do you constantly scroll through e-mails in your Inbox?

If you happened to answer Yes to any or all three of the questions (OMG) above, you might want to reconsider how you work.

Every time you scroll up or down (Processing information), you waste time that could have been used to accomplish a task (Produce work.)

Instead, when you look at an e-mail, make a decision and move it to one of four places: FADS.

- Forward it to someone.
- Drag it to an Action folder you created in the window on the left.
- Delete it.
- Save it to one of your Support Category folders in Windows Explorer.

Remember, Scroll is not Norwegian for "To your health!" It is the computer word for "Wasting time!"

120

Include your name and phone number when sending e-mail.

How many times have you received an e-mail and needed to clarify something that would take too long to type, but could be accomplished in a quarter of the time with a call? But there wasn't any phone number on the e-mail to call.

You can Google their number, call directory assistance, waste a lot of time trying to explain what you need to say through a lengthy return e-mail, or not call at all. Or, they could just have added their phone number to their e-mail and saved everyone a lot of time.

You never know. You just might start receiving those calls that you have been waiting for.

Sometimes it just makes sense—and saves a lot more time—to call.

121

Set up a Signature for your e-mails.

Are you tired of having to type in your name and number at the bottom of every e-mail you send?

Never again. Here's how to set up a Signature in Outlook 2013:

1. Open Outlook 2013.
2. Click on the File tab on the Ribbon on the top.
3. On the left side, click on Options.
4. An Outlook Options dialogue box will appear.
5. Click on Mail on the left.
6. Click on the Signatures button on the right.
7. A Signatures and Stationery dialogue box will appear.
8. Click on the E-mail Signature tab if it is not selected.
9. Click the New button.
10. A New Signature dialogue box will appear with a blinking cursor.
11. Type in a name that you will call the signature.

12. In the large box on the bottom, under Edit Signature, type in what you want your signature to be such as:
    - Your name
    - Your company
    - Your phone number
    - Your e-mail address
    - Your web page
13. Now go to the top right under Choose default signature.
14. You can add your new signature to both New messages and Replies/forwards by clicking on the arrows to the right with the specified signature. Various e-mail signatures will appear if you have more than one. Click on the one you want.
15. If you have more than one e-mail, make sure you have it selected in the E-mail account box above that.
16. Click OK.

♫Signed. Sealed. Delivered. I'm yours.♫

122

Forward an e-mail–the safe way.

Do you ever wonder why you get viruses or junk mail? Could it possibly be because of how you forward e-mails?

No way!

Way!

Every time you Forward an e-mail, there is information left over from the people who got the messages before you—their e-mail address and name. As the messages are Forwarded along, the list of addresses builds. When some poor guy gets a virus, his computer will send that virus to every e-mail address that has come across his computer.

Instead, do the following:

1. When you Forward an e-mail, delete all of the other addresses that appear in the body of the message (at the top). You must click the Forward button first and then you

will have full editing capabilities with the body and headers of the message.

2. Whenever you send an e-mail to more than one person, do not use the To or Cc fields for adding e-mail addresses. Always use the Bcc (blind carbon copy) field for listing the e-mail addresses. If you don't see the Bcc option, click on where it says To and your address list will appear. Highlight the address and choose Bcc. When you send using Bcc your message will automatically say 'Undisclosed Recipients' in the To field of the people who receive it.

3. Remove any 'FW:' in the subject line. You can also change the Subject if you wish. Just make sure to hit the Save icon. (This is also helpful when you use Bcc to create an extra copy for yourself to save. Eliminating the 'FW' will allow you to find the file alphabetically.)

4. Always hit your Forward button from the actual e-mail you are reading.

This is a great way to stop junk mail and viruses.

Now this is an example of something that should be Forwarded.

123

Scrolling = Producing nothing.

How many times do you scroll over the same e-mails in your Inbox? Some e-mails have been there for so long that they are grandfathered in.

Many people have made checking their e-mails a big part of their job—and then can't seem to understand why they don't get more done.

Who knows, there may be a job in the future as an e-mail viewer.

"What do you do?"

"I scroll through e-mails "

"Do you work on them?"

"No. I just look at them. That's my job."

In your dreams, buddy. That would be a wonderful job as long as someone else worked on the e-mails.

Wherever you keep your e-mails, one thing is for sure, it better not be in your Inbox.

The next time you see those old e-mails, tell them to go away… that you never want to see them again.

124

Rules Schmules.

Have you set up a Rule in Outlook so that all e-mails that come from a particular source are sent to a specified folder?

That's great if you go through the folder regularly and read and delete the e-mails. It's not if you are one of the people who just send them off to La-la folder land and then never look at them again. That means build up. Big build up. Not good.

Instead, have all e-mails come through your Inbox so you are forced to make a decision with each one. Don't be afraid to delete them if you find you aren't doing anything with them. You know the ones I am talking about.

Do not have them automatically dragged, kicking and screaming, to a folder never again to be looked at.

Do 'em or delete 'em.

125

Move all of your Support saved e-mails to Windows Explorer.

Do you have too many folders in your e-mail program? When you aren't sure of where to file something, do you just create another folder?

You can clean out all of your non-action e-mails and store them in one place. Here's how:

1. Open Windows Explorer and Outlook.

2. Right click an open space on your Taskbar which is at the bottom of the page.
3. A drop down box that goes up appears.
4. Click on Show windows side by side.
5. Both an Outlook and Windows Explorer window will appear on your screen, one on the left and the other on the right.
6. Now for the good part. Select the e-mail in Outlook you want to save. Left click it and drag and drop the e-mail to the Support Category folder in your Windows Explorer/My Documents window.
7. If the folder that you want to save the e-mail in isn't open, just hold the e-mail over the folder above it and it will open it.

This will save your e-mail as an e-mail with its attachments. Since it is still an e-mail, you can reference the information, Forward the e-mail, or reply to the e-mail.

Suddenly, there are only tasks to do (Action) in your e-mail program. Makes it kind of easy to know what to do now, doesn't it?

Hallelujah!

126

Save your e-mails to Windows Explorer by using .msg.

Do you have Support files (files you save and refer to) in both Windows Explorer and in your e-mail program? Why would you want to waste time looking for files in two places?

Save your Support (non-Action) e-mails to Windows Explorer so all of your files are in one location on your computer. Here's how in Microsoft Outlook 2013:

1. Open the e-mail.
2. Go to the File tab on the top left corner of your screen on the Ribbon and click it. A new page will open.
3. Click on Save As.
4. A Save As dialogue box will appear.
5. Select the Category you want to save the file in under Libraries>Documents>My Documents.

6. Type in the file name.
7. Click on the down arrow in the bottom box labeled: Save as type.
8. Select Outlook Message Format (*.msg).
9. Click on the Save button.

By saving your e-mail in this format, when you go to Windows Explorer/My Documents to find the file, it will be in the form of an e-mail. This allows you to reference the information, Forward it, or reply to it since it is still an e-mail.

Sweet!

127

Create icons on your Quick Access Toolbar to save clicks.

Are you one of those people who are stuck in a click? Maybe it's time you got out.

Having an icon on your Quick Access Toolbar means clicking just once instead of multiple times. Here's how to add one in Outlook 2013:

1. Open Outlook.
2. Go to the Quick Access Toolbar on the top.
3. Click on the mini down arrow on the far right side of the Quick Access Toolbar.
4. A drop down menu will appear.
5. Click on More Commands.
6. Click on Quick Access Toolbar on the left if it isn't already selected.
7. There will be a right and left box.
8. Above the left box, under Choose commands from, click on the down arrow on the right side.
9. A drop down menu will appear.
10. Click on All Commands.
11. Scroll through to locate the icons that you want to add to the Quick Access Toolbar.
12. Click on one of the icons in the left box such as Copy.
13. Then click on the Add>> button in between the two boxes.

14. This will add the Copy icon to the list in the right box under Customize Quick Access Toolbar.
15. Select all of the icons you want to add to the Quick Access Toolbar.
16. When finished selecting the icons, click the OK button.

No more, here a click, there a click, everywhere a click-click.

One icon. One click.

128

Use these icons on your Quick Access Toolbar.

Now that you are saving time by using icons on your Quick Access Toolbar in Outlook 2013, which ones should you move up and use?

Here they are:

Address book	Bottom (Reading Pane)
Calendar	Contacts
Copy	Cut
Delete	Empty Deleted Items
Forward	Junk E-mail Options
Move to Folder	New Contact
New Folder	New Email
New Post in This Folder	Paste
Print	Reply
Right (Reading Pane)	Save All Attachments
Save As	Select All
Show in Groups	Undo

Of course you can add any others that you use.

One click shopping.

129

Use your To-Do Bar so your Calendar and appointments are visible.

Did you know that in Outlook 2013, you have a To-Do Bar that is actually a Calendar with a list of appointments? Here's how to open it:

1. Open Microsoft Outlook 2013.
2. Click on the View tab on the Ribbon at the top. A grouping of icons will appear.
3. Click on the To-Do Bar icon in the Layout group. As you do, a drop-down box will appear.
4. Click only on Calendar (not on People or Tasks).

Suddenly, on the right side of your screen, a new window will appear which is your To-Do Bar (Calendar). You can view any date in the current month with just one click on the date. In addition, a listing of your appointments will appear under the Calendar.

Seeing is believing.

130

Keep an extra e-mail to manipulate by using a Bcc.

When you send an e-mail, do you ever want to keep a copy of it so you can have it when you need it?

If so, create a Bcc (Blind carbon copy). Oops! Make that a visually impaired C based duplicate. Here's how in Outlook 2013.

1. On the Ribbon on the top, click on the Home tab.
2. In the New Group, click on the New E-mail icon.
3. Click on where it says Bcc.
4. Type in your e-mail address.

There are many ways to use Bcc to your advantage. One is drag the duplicate e-mail to the Calendar icon on a specific date for a meeting or call. Remember that same e-mail was sent to the person you have a meeting or call with. This enables you to have that information available on that date. (It's always good to have the facts.)

Or after you send an e-mail, the Bcc can act as a reminder for you to work on something in preparation for a meeting. Move the Bcc e-mail to the To Do A folder to work on. When completed, drag it to the meeting date on the Calendar so you will have it available. The possibilities are almost endless.

Nobody likes to be manipulated, except maybe an e-mail.

131

Completely clean out your Inbox by creating a temporary one.

Do you have a hard time completely emptying your e-mail Inbox because you have so many e-mails in it? Wouldn't you really like a fresh start with an empty Inbox?

Here's how to create a second, temporary Inbox in your e-mail program.

1. Open Microsoft Outlook 2013.
2. In the Folder Pane on the left, select the Inbox folder.
3. Go to the top of the page on the Ribbon and select the Folder tab.
4. Click on the New Folder icon.
5. A dialogue box will appear. Type in "_Inbox2" In the open space.
6. Hit OK. The folder will now appear below your existing Inbox folder.

Now for the good part. You are going to move all of your current e-mails to this temporary Inbox. If you have a lot of e-mails (thousands), you may want to do this at the end of the day as it may take hours to download them.

1. Left click the top e-mail in your Inbox. Hold down the Shift key. Go down to the last e-mail and click on it. (All of your e-mails should be selected.)
2. Grab any e-mail (left click it and hold it down) and drag it to the _Inbox2 folder. Let it go.

3. All of your e-mails will be moved (or soon will be) to your new _Inbox2 folder.

Congratulations! You now have an empty Inbox and can start deciding (emptying it) on it three times a day.

What do you do with all of the old e-mails that you have moved? Clean out a few from the top (the most current ones) when you go through your regular Inbox three times a day. Eventually you will get rid of all of them.

Don't screw it up again (by not deciding) or the same thing will happen.

132

Reply to your e-mail messages later.

Would you change how you do your e-mail if you could cut the time you spent on it in half?

When someone e-mails you and asks a question, what do you normally do? Answer them—right then. Not, however, if you want to cut the time that you spend going through them in half.

In Microsoft Outlook 2013, create a folder called Reply under your Batched Action folder in the Folder Pane on the left. Rather than replying to your e-mails when you read them, drag them to the Reply folder. Later, after you have finished Processing (categorizing, sorting, prioritizing) all of your e-mails, you can go back to the Reply folder and reply to all of them.

Incredibly, by not replying to them immediately but batching and doing them at the same time, you will cut the time you spend on them in half.

Step right up. We have a winner.

133

Save an e-mail with its attachments to a specific date.

Where do you keep an e-mail you need for a specific meeting? Don't you dare say your Inbox.

You can keep an e-mail with attachments you need for an appointment in your Outlook 2013 Calendar. However, if you try to drag it to the Calendar icon, you'll lose the attachment. Here's how not to:

1. Select the e-mail.
2. Click on the Home tab on the Ribbon on the top
3. Next click on the Move icon in the Move group. A drop down list will appear.
4. Click on Other folders.
5. Click on Calendar.
6. An appointment screen will appear.
7. Set the date by clicking on the Start time date down arrow.
8. A mini-calendar will appear. Click on the desired date.
9. For a specific appointment time, click on the Time down arrow.
10. Select Save and Close.

The e-mail will appear at your appointment time on that date when you click the Day Calendar button on the Menu bar. You can open the e-mail and review its contents and attachments for your meeting by simply clicking on it.

You look so much smarter when you have all of the facts!

134

Stop incoming e-mail notifications from appearing on your screen.

Is your computer haunted (and interrupted) by mysterious messages fading in and out on the lower right side of your screen?

Every alert is an unnecessary interruption. Here is how to turn off all e-mail alerts:

1. Open an e-mail in Microsoft Outlook 2013.
2. Click on the File tab on the Ribbon on the top left.
3. Click on Options on the left.
4. An Outlook Options dialogue box will open up.
5. Click on Mail on the left.
6. Go down to Message Arrival.
7. Uncheck all four boxes.
8. Click on the OK button.

As the woman in Poltergeist said, "This screen is clean."

135

Edit your e-mails to include an action that you just took.

Did you know that you can edit and add information to an existing e-mail?

Editing an e-mail allows you to note any conversations you had, any phone messages you left, any updates you want to include, or a reminder of an action you need to take, right on the e-mail itself eliminating the need to note it somewhere else.

Here's how in Microsoft Outlook 2013:

1. Open the e-mail.
2. Click on the Message tab on the Ribbon on the top left.
3. In the Move group area, click on Actions. A drop down box will magically appear.
4. Click on Edit message. This allows you to make changes to the e-mail.
5. Move the cursor to where you want to type.
6. Type in the action you need to take regarding the e-mail, or the information you want to note, preferably on the top of the page as it is easier to see there.
7. Click on the Save button which is all the way on the top left of your screen on the Quick Access Toolbar.

Ladies and gentlemen, start your editing.

136

See attachments easily.

Don't you just hate having to double click an e-mail attachment to find out what's in it?

Double click no more. From now on, a single click will do ya'. Here's how in Microsoft Outlook 2013.

With the Right Reading Pane view on:

1. Go to the e-mail that has the attachment.
2. In the open window on the right, left click the attachment one time.

With the Bottom Reading Pane view on:

1. Go to the e-mail that has the attachment.
2. In the open window on the bottom, left click the attachment one time.

By the way, never have the Reading Pane turned to the Off position so the e-mails are in a list format.

Use either the Right or Bottom view depending on your e-mail program version. Otherwise, you may develop a bad case of Scroll-itis (the incessant urge to constantly scroll up and down).

Open sesame.

137

Tap your way into seeing your files on the Taskbar.

Do you normally work with a lot of files open at the same time? With so many open at the same time, is it difficult to find a specific file?

Wouldn't it be nice to have all of your open files lined up horizontally across your screen so you could see each one with a simple tap?

Just hold the Windows 7 button down and tap the Tab key until you find the file you are looking for. Then release. When you release, the file that was in the front or on the right, will open to a full panoramic screen.

In Windows 8 hold the Windows button and Alt button down, and tap the Tab key.

I can see you!

138

Occasionally bigger is better.

Is the font size of the letters on your outgoing e-mail too small?

If so, the following is a magic growth formula to increase the size of the letters:

1. Open Microsoft Outlook 2013
2. On the Ribbon on top, click on the File tab.
3. Click on Options.
4. Click on Mail.
5. Click on the Signatures button.
6. Click on the Personal Stationery tab.
7. Click on the Font button.
8. Click on the Font tab (New Mail message).
9. Go to Size: and change the font size as big (or as little) as you want.
10. Click the OK button.

♫Who's afraid of the big bad font?♫

139

Create your very own Tab in Outlook.

Do you find yourself clicking from Tab to Tab on the Ribbon on top trying to find commonly used icons? Wouldn't it be easier if all of the action icons you frequently used were on a single Tab?

Here's how to create that one Tab in Microsoft Outlook 2013. The best part is, you get to name the Tab anything you want. Hint: Your name.

1. Right click an existing Tab on top such as the Home tab.
2. A drop down menu will appear. Click on Customize the Ribbon.
3. A Word Options dialogue box will appear. On the left, click on Customize Ribbon.
4. Go to the bottom right and click on the New Tab button.
5. A New Tab (Custom) will appear. Select it.
6. Click the Rename button. A Rename dialogue box will appear.
7. Type in the name of the new Tab.
8. Hit OK.
9. Then go to the bottom and hit the OK button.

You can move the location of the Tab on the top to the left or to the right of the page by selecting the Tab and clicking on the Up or Down arrow on the right.

One maybe the loneliest number but it sure saves a lot of Tab time.

140

Set up your default.

Aren't you tired of the endless clicking?

I am talking about having to click a zillion times when you want to save a new Microsoft Word 2013 document to your shared drive in Windows Explorer Here's how to cut down on the clicks:

1. Open up Microsoft Word 2013.
2. Click the File Tab on the top left of the Ribbon.
3. Click on Options.
4. Click on Save.
5. Under the Save Documents heading, click the box in front of "Save to Computer by default."
6. Under that, go to "Default local file location:"
7. Click on the Browse button to find the folder that you want to appear.
8. Hit OK.

The next time you open a new Word document and hit the Save As button, you will be magically transported to the folder of your dreams with all of your Support Category folders under it. Click on the Category folder and then type in the file name in the box below.

Hey. Default is yours if you don't use it.

141

Use the Bottom Reading Pane when going through e-mail.

Is your Reading Pane view turned to Off so that you have a long list of e-mails to scroll through in your Inbox? Please don't tell me that your Message or Auto Preview is also on.

In Microsoft Outlook 2013, by using the Bottom Reading Pane and keeping the horizontal split bar almost all of the way to the top on the right window (you can move it by grabbing it with your mouse and dragging it up), or the Right Reading Pane, you can scan your messages one at a time, decide where they go and then drag the message to one of the following places: FADS: Forward, Action, Delete, Support (or Save).

Here is how to open the Bottom or Right Reading Pane:
1. Click on the View tab on the Ribbon on the top.
2. In the Layout group, click on Reading Pane.
3. Click on Bottom or Right.

Set them up (e-mails) one at a time. Then knock them out, one at a time.

Save yourself a pain by using the correct Reading Pane.

142

Use the Right Reading Pane when working from your Action folders.

What would happen if you kept all of your to-do's in only one place? Say in Action folders in your e-mail program? Could you find everything you needed to work on quicker than where they are now?

Winning the Productivity Game

In Microsoft Outlook 2013, by using the Right Reading Pane view, you are able to see a list of all of the tasks you need to work on by folder. It is kind of like a to-do list except all of the tasks listed in a folder are categorized by a common type of action (such as Read, Call, Pay, etc.). It is very different from the wide range of tasks you normally would have on your to-do list or in your Inbox.

Here is how to open the Right Reading Pane:

1. Click on the View tab on the Ribbon on top.
2. In the Layout group, click on Reading Pane.
3. Click on Right.

For all of you to-do list fanatics that will never give up your lists, fear not, you can still keep them. But now in a more effective way.

143

Create shortcut icons for your software programs on your Taskbar.

Do you ever find yourself wasting time trying to open a software program? You can go to the Start button, then All Programs, and then click on a Program, or you can go to your desktop to open them each time. Or you can just click an icon once on the Taskbar. Here's how:

1. Left click on the round Start icon on the far left side of the Taskbar.
2. Left click on All Programs.
3. Scroll to the Program you want to have available.
4. Left click the Program and drag (hold it down) and drop it down onto the Taskbar.
5. You will see a message that says "Pin to Taskbar."

If the icon is on your desktop, and you drag it to the Taskbar, you can delete the icon on your desktop as you will never need to open it from there again.

To get rid of an icon, simply right click the icon. Then click on "Unpin this program from Taskbar."

Quick! Launch your shortcuts!

144

Rename the Subject line of an e-mail.

Did you know that you can change what is written in the Subject line of any e-mail?

Here's how in Microsoft Outlook 2013:

1. Open the e-mail.
2. Go to the Subject box at the top and select the written type.
3. Type in a new subject.
4. Click on the Save button which is on the Quick Access Toolbar on the top left of your screen.

Changing the Subject line to more accurate or familiar words will allow you to quickly and easily identify what the e-mail is about especially when viewing it in the Right Reading Pane view.

Changing it is especially beneficial if you have updated it or the status of the e-mail has changed.

Hey you change your oil. Why not your Subject line?

145

Use the F12 key for when you need to use Save As.

Question: What are the least number of clicks needed to save an e-mail or a document?

Answer: One.

The next time you want to save something, just hit the F12 key.

By the way, there are 11 other F keys you can use to be productive.

Who loves you, baby?

146

Using Search versus using a good filing system

Which works better? Older or newer technology? The answer seems kind of obvious, but is it?

Years ago, there was a contest on a late night TV show to see which technology could send information quicker. One team texted while the other used Morse code. No contest right? Wrong! The Morse code team won. Newer technology isn't always faster—or better.

I am guessing that most people would say that using Search in their e-mail program would allow them to find information quicker than using a good filing system. Not always.

Using a good organizational system allows you to find information in a couple of seconds. With some Search programs, every single e-mail (with the word(s) that you entered) will come up. Many times that can be a lot of e-mails to have to look through and a lot of times it takes more than a couple of seconds to find it.

Should you never use the Search button? Of course not. There are many times it can be used very efficiently. But if you happen to be one of those people who save every e-mail that was ever sent to you in your Inbox, don't expect to find everything in a couple of seconds.

You can expect to, however, if you use the right information storage system.

147

Color is the quickest and easiest way for you to organize anything.

When you first meet someone, how do you initially size them up? Isn't it visually?

The same principle is true in your office. The first way you organize anything is visually.

Colors are the easiest way to remember your Categories (a grouping of similar or like things). When I see the color blue, I think of a Category called "Forms," since filling out forms always depresses me and makes me blue. Green for "Financial" and money. Orange for "PR," since Anita Bryant was the PR person for Florida orange juice years ago. You don't have to use these—you get to make your own weird associations.

Let the color "tip you off" as to what the Category is.

148

To the right, ever to the right.

Q: In a file drawer, should the plastic tabs on the hanging folders be lined up in the far left lane alphabetically and front to back, or should they be staggered across from the left to the right, alphabetically?

A: Front to the back, even though they are easier to read when they are staggered. The reason you don't stagger the tabs is because every time you add a new tab, you will have to move and adjust all of the other tabs.

Think about a file drawer looking at it from the front to the back. Here are the rules for tab placement:

- A to Z. Alphabetically going from the front to the back.

- Left to right. Tabs always start on the far left lane going to the right with the general on the left and the more specific as you move to the right.

- When you have too much information in a hanging folder and you want to find the information quicker, you can break it down into hanging folders directly behind the hanging folder and a tab lane to the right.

- When you move a tab over, it is always one full tab (1/5 tab) to the right so that if all five tabs were spread out, each tab would be fully visible.

By the way, tabs go on the inside front of a hanging folder not the inside back. Doing it this way eliminates an extra wasted motion. The next time you are bored with nothing to do, try it.

149

Keep a tax due date list.

How many times have you missed a tax payment because you forgot about the due date? How much of a penalty did you have to pay? Bet you really enjoyed paying that!

The following is an example of a partial list of tax due dates for Georgia. Personalize it (consult with a CPA for yours) and then use it to remind yourself of those special dates that you get to give more money to the government (accompanying high pitched screams are okay).

Due date: Taxes Due:

Jan 20   Sales and use tax (high volume needs to be filed monthly)
Jan 31   Quarterly payroll tax returns
    Year-end payroll tax returns
    1099s due to individuals
    W2s due to individuals
March 15   Corporate income tax returns
March 31   Business License (due date tends to vary by state and locality)
April 1   Personal property tax
    Corporation renewal registration fee
April 15   Individual income tax returns
    Partnership income tax returns
April 30   Quarterly payroll tax returns
July 31   Quarterly payroll tax returns
Sept 15   Corporate income tax returns extended due date
    Partnership income tax returns extended due date
Oct 15   Personal income tax returns extended due date
Oct 31   Quarterly payroll tax returns

In Outlook, copy the list to a New Post in This Folder card. Then drag it to the Outlook calendar. Simply move it from date to date in your calendar to remind you of the payment due date.

In a paper system, copy the dates to a 3x5 card. Move it from date to date in your hanging folders (Calendar system) to remind you of the payment due date.

Believe me. The last thing you want to do is to get to know the IRS more intimately.

150

Use the date of service as the invoice number.

What do you do if you generally don't use an invoice number and need one? How can you make the number relevant to what you sold?

You can use a secret numbering system started by an ancient civilization that visited Earth three thousand years ago. Or you can just use the date of the service as the number.

For example: 070415 means July 4, 2015. The first two numbers are the month, the next two are the date, and the last two the year. By adding a letter to the end of the number, you can further expand its meaning. For example I means in state and O means out of state.

By using this system, you will always have a logical way to tie the invoice to the date of service.

Congratulations! Your number has finally come up.

151

Break down tax deductions by subject.

It's March. Have you finished your taxes? What? You haven't started them yet?

April 15th will be here before you know it. What are you waiting for? Send your money in. The government needs money to pay for their $5,000 hammers. Next year's returns will be due before you know it.

Here are two easy ways to get more organized for Tax time:

1. (Computer) Create an Excel spreadsheet with the specific types of deductions listed down the far left column. List each tax year along the top from the left (current year) to the right (next year). This allows you to compare your current year amount with other years. During the year, when you pay an amount such as your Ad Valorum tax for your car, you can type in the amount in its spot. Then later, use the rest of the form as a reminder for all of the other important numbers you need to type in.

2. (Paper) Have a Support Category called Accounts Paid. This is where all invoices you have paid are filed. Title each hanging folder by its subject such as: Medical, Childcare, Insurance, etc. At the end of the year, total the invoices in each folder and you have the amount spent for each taxable area.

Thinking about tax time reminds me of one of my favorite Christmas lyrics: "It's the most, wonderful time of the year."

Not.

152

All paper should be kept in only one room in your home.

How many places do you keep paper in your house? Any stuffed in that cubbyhole in your kitchen? Any piled on your desk in your study? Any plastered all over your poor, defenseless refrigerator? Hey, the poor thing can hardly breathe. Take some off.

The goal is to store all of your paper in only one place in your home, preferably in an office or an extra bedroom—never in the bedroom where you sleep. Not only is it energetically healthier to store all your paper in only one place, but it's also easier to find things.

Come out, come out, wherever you are, you little hidden pieces of papers you.

153

Junk your Junk Drawer.

Admit it. You've got one. So does everyone else. A Junk Drawer!

You know, that drawer that you put stuff into with items that you don't know what to do with.

Well, I've got some bad news for you. It's getting bigger—and has probably started spreading to other drawers. Someday in the near future, all your drawers may turn to the dark side and become—Darth Drawers.

There's a New Hope. Go to that drawer and completely empty it. Then wipe it completely out using a rag and cleaning agent. Give that drawer a new name (Category) and vow from now on to put only like items that belong together in it.

Now for the fun part. Go through every item in the drawer and make a decision as to where to put each item. Categorize everything and either save each item to the appropriate location, give it away, or trash it (about 60% will be trash).

Save the Rainforests of Endor. Eliminate the Junk Drawers.

154

Keep a basket at the top and the bottom of the stairs.

Where do you put items that need to go upstairs when you are downstairs?

From now on, place a basket at the top and the bottom of your stairs. When you have something you need to take upstairs, instead of having to walk it up right then, leave it on the stairs, or just forget about it, you can just drop it into a basket. When you go upstairs, grab what's in the basket and drop it into an Inbox up there.

It's the same process for taking something downstairs. Just drop it in the basket and the next time you are going down, grab it.

I know this has its ups and downs, but at least you won't become a basket case over it.

155

All household mail goes into your home Inbox.

When you bring your mail in, where do you put it? The dining room table? The hutch in the kitchen? Any open surfaces you can find which are disappearing faster than the ozone layer?

Instead, drop the mail into an Inbox along with any other papers. That way, your papers won't be scattered from your garage to the top of the refrigerator. Believe it or not, you get to dump all that mail in it all week long without having to do anything with it until Saturday when you get to go through it. Use OATS (Outbox, Action, Trash, Support or Save) to distribute the contents.

If it is in your Inbox, it won't be anywhere else.

Late breaking news: It's also okay to have a home Outbox. Your Outbox is a great place to leave your keys or anything else you need to take with you when you leave the house. Just check it every time before you leave and you'll never forget anything.

That was easy!

156

Got stuff?

Does the thought of venturing into your basement terrify you? When down there viewing the motley number of items, does that spooky voice in your head ever whisper any of the following?

1. I can always use it for parts.
2. It's hard to get these anymore.
3. I always wanted one of these when I was a kid.
4. I am going to learn how to use this someday.
5. I know I can fix this.
6. This is going to be worth a lot in the future.

7. It was a gift.
8. We vacationed there. I just couldn't throw it away.
9. I am sure they will be back in style soon.
10. Dad made this for me.
11. You've got to have at least one of these for a backup.
12. I just know the kids will want these someday.

Are you saving stuff for a legitimate reason or are you just not dealing with it?

Maybe it's time to start dealing.

157

Every piece of paper has energy

Have you ever considered that a piece of paper is full of energy? Or perhaps full of something else?

Each piece of paper has its own energy—sometimes positive, sometimes negative. The energy depends on what you decide to do or not do with it.

Think about a project you have procrastinated working on that is buried under a pile of papers stacked in the corner of your bedroom. You think that puppy is giving off positive vibes? Hardly! It's like a black hole, sucking in all the surrounding energy. Oh! That's where Spot went.

Think the concept of energy is bogus? Think about how you would feel with your eyes closed, standing in a dirty, cluttered house. Yuck! Then compare that with the feeling of being in a newly built, clean house. Ah! You can feel the difference yet scientifically you can't prove it. Yet it's all about the energy.

When you finally go through and deal with those stacks of paper that soon may turn into your very own Petrified Forest, you'll notice a feeling as if a weight has been lifted from you.

It has.

158

Read a page a day.

After graduating from High School, 15% of the population will never read a book again. Are you so busy that you can't find time to read?

Pick out a favorite book of yours and place it on your night stand. Every night before you go to bed, read a page. That's it. Just one page. This strenuous and exhausting task may take you all of a minute to do. Worse, it could deprive you of a minute of your highly sought after sleep but rest assured, it will be well worth it. At the end of a year, you will have completed a 365-page book that you never would have read.

"Once upon a time, there was a busy person who believed they didn't have any time to read…but really did…and they lived happily ever after."

159

Your Inbox will be with you for a long time.

Want to hear something really scary?

For the rest of your life, as long as someone is sending you information, you will need to go through some sort of an Inbox… and hopefully that will be for a very long time. Additionally, you will need to go through your desk Inbox at least until you stop receiving paper and mail.

Isn't it time you learned how to do it quickly and effectively—since you will be doing it for the rest of your life?

The key to quickly and completely emptying your Inbox is to decide where it goes, and then drag it or move it there. Never, ever, do it.

Move it. Then groove it.

Greg Vetter

160

You are the biggest cause of your interruptions.

Who do you think interrupts you more than anyone else? Bingo! Pick one from the top shelf.

Think how many times you interrupt yourself by responding to an e-mail when it annoyingly announces itself. Actually, I would prefer hearing Chopin's funeral dirge rather than that annoying ding. Instead, what the e-mail should say is "I am interrupting you yet once again. Are you going to take the bait, look at me, then leave me in your Inbox, or start working on me, which will interrupt what you were just working on? Or will you finally, once and for all, ignore me and check me later?"

Believe it or not, you don't have to look at every single e-mail every single time when they come in. Really!

All these years, you may have believed it was other people who were interrupting you. They probably have, but give yourself some credit too! Over 50% of your interruptions are caused by or allowed by you.

How long are you willing to work without interrupting yourself?

The bucks stop coming when you keep interrupting!

161

It's time for a Time Out for your kids.

How many days a week are your kids involved in an activity? Congratulations! You might be turning them into a Mini-you.

A more humane question might be how many days aren't they doing something.

Kids average five hours a day on media. That is a far cry from a TV set with aluminum lined rabbit ears that could only get three channels. And, that doesn't even include daily activity time.

Down time for a kid is like Quiet Time for an adult. If neither gets it, bad things occur.

Reality check: Take a look at your life. See anyone near and dear whose life is beginning to look like yours?

Be careful of what you are teaching your kids. They will learn it better than you ever thought.

They're watching you.

162

Work on only one task at a time.

Everyone knows that multitasking makes you more productive, right? Except it's not true.

Most of the time your brain isn't multitasking—it's toggling back and forth between tasks at a super-fast speed that feels as if you are actually multitasking.

Research has shown that it takes a person 50 percent longer to complete two tasks done simultaneously than if the tasks were worked on separately. Huh?

Let me get this straight. If I work on one task, it will take me ten minutes to complete it. If I work on two ten-minute tasks at the same time, it will take me 30 minutes to complete them. Didn't I lose ten minutes doing it this way? Wasn't it supposed to take less than 20 minutes?

So how many other things are you doing while you are reading this?"

163

How to stay focused on one task.

How many tasks do you work on at the same time?

I know they say multitasking will make you more productive but nothing is farther from the truth.

What happens when an e-mail arrives? You stop what you're doing, interrupt yourself, and open the e-mail while working on other things. Then you kind of just let the e-mail sit in your Inbox still needing to be dealt with later—along with everything else that you stopped working on.

If you analyze your behavior, you'll notice that you are constantly shifting from Processing information to Producing work—back and forth all day long, with the sneaking feeling of never really completing anything.

Working on one thing is not only more productive, it will also improve the quality of your work life. Imagine that.

If you want to juggle things so badly, join the circus!

164

Turn off all alerts, cues and vibrations on your devices.

How many times a day do you think an average person checks an electronic device?

Again, an average of 150 times. Most people don't realize that when they are checking a device, they aren't producing work. Checking e-mail is a great example of this.

If you are constantly checking a device and allowing yourself to be interrupted, when will you get any work done?

Accomplishing work is what your goal is, not checking the status of _____. (Fill in the blank with all of the things you check.)

When you are Processing information (checking devices), you aren't Producing work (creating results).

Let's hope you don't buy any more electronic devices that need to be checked.

165

Know thy key activity.

Do you know what the most important and impactful activity you can do in your job is? (Showing up for work doesn't count.)

Who do you think would understand this question better? A Fortune 100 executive or a small business entrepreneur? Sadly, neither. After doing Executive Focus Coaching for more than 25 years, I have found very few workers have ever taken the time to discover this key activity. And the few that have, generally don't use it to their advantage.

Think about this: What is the one activity that you can do that will cause the most positive and beneficial impact that will greatly increase your work output?

When you discover this, the impact you make will be staggering and your work life will change in a way that you can't comprehend.

So what is it?

166

Important and Urgent are not the same.

Do you use important and urgent interchangeably? You are not alone. Most people today confuse urgent with important. Luckily, you can be one of the few to differentiate between them by following these rules:

- Urgent is strictly time-based.
- Important is impact-based.

A task can be important and have a due date. A task can also just be very important with no time frame to be accomplished. This is called a Priority.

Notice how much less stress you experience when you stop treating them the same.

167

Your priorities stay the same.

How often do your priorities change? Weekly? Daily? Hourly?

Priorities rarely change. Urgencies, on the other hand, constantly change. Many people confuse urgencies with priorities.

A priority is one thing that, when focused on and with a majority of time spent on, creates the most bang for your buck.

Priorities generally don't change. It is the time-based Urgencies that do.

Next time recognize what you may think is a priority, for what it really is—an urgency.

168

Prioritize, rather than Urgentize or Easinize your tasks.

Are you prioritizing your tasks? Or are you really just urgentizing and easinizing them?

Try this: Pick out the first tasks that you would work on from a list of things to do. Most people don't realize that they unconsciously look for due dates when they "prioritize" their work. That's not prioritizing—it's urgentizing. Tasks with a due date often have nothing to do with being a priority.

Others look for the easiest tasks so that at the end of the day, they can experience a sense of having accomplished a lot. Perhaps— but at the cost of not working on their important tasks—and it's a fleeting feeling.

A priority is not necessarily urgent or easy. It is simply the most important and impactful task that you can work on. Many times it is the least worked on.

Prioritize, Urgentize or Easinize? It's your choice.

169

Be a fire marshal rather than a fire fighter.

In today's frantic work environment, does it seem fair that the fire fighter rather than the fire marshal gets rewarded?

If you are constantly reacting to the same emergencies and putting out the same type of recurring fires, something is rotten—or I should say "burning" in Denmark.

Instead of you having to always fight the same fires, why not put them out once and for all? Go back and look at the patterns that occur. Then create permanent solutions and implement them.

Spot the fires before they start or your job description will soon include being a part-time fireman.

Do this now before there are too many fires to be able to put out.

170

Many important tasks do not have a due date.

Do you believe that if a task doesn't have a due date or deadline, it can't be very important?

Many people do. Yet nothing could be further from the truth. Many of your most impactful activities will never have a due date. These are the activities you never seem to have time for but in reality, are most essential for the continued success of your business. These are the tasks that drive your organization to success.

Continue to ignore these "dateless wonders" and watch what happens to your company in the future.

You may just end up driving your organization into the ditch.

Greg Vetter

171

If you have too much on your plate, tip it.

When was the last time you spent a quiet evening at home?

With information doubling, our personal RAM at a saturation point, being connected 24/7, and trying to fit more activities into our weekly schedule than a contestant on Supermarket Sweep tries to stuff into their shopping cart, it's time to stop.

We've done a magnificent job of overcomplicating our already overcomplicated lives. Simplify. Do less. Disconnect. Unplug. Take that smartphone ear plug out before it becomes permanently attached.

"Be" for a while, instead of always "Doing." Waste some time. (Gulp! Did I say that?) Slow down; your life will be over soon enough. It's going by a lot faster than you think. You are no longer 25.

The only items that will fall off are the ones that are supposed to.

Now take a deep breath and tip that plate.

172

Set up your day around your key activity.

Why do you have time for reactive tasks yet never time for important ones?

Most people spend their day reacting to e-mails, Tweets, calls, texts, deadlines, urgencies, and sometimes whims rather than pro-acting and setting their day up around their key activity.

Plan your day around your key activity. Then watch everything else magically fall into place.

By the way, do you know what your key activity is?

173

Work on your key activity first.

How many key activities do you have?

If "key" is singular and "activities" is plural, then something doesn't match.

Many people think they have a bunch of key activities. What if they only have one?

Remember the movie City Slickers with Billy Crystal? Curly the Trail Boss (Jack Palance) knew this secret. As he held up his forefinger, he said it was all about one thing, but you had to figure out what that one thing was.

At work, there is one thing you always need to be working on first, and when you do, somehow everything else seems to fall into place.

What is that one thing for you?

Yee-hah!

174

Follow the flow.

Remember having to sit at a desk for 6 hours as a kid in school? Did you ever think you were going to have to repeat that same type of idiotic behavior when you grew up and got a job? Surprise!

Who came up with the idea that your day was supposed to be so completely crammed with appointments, work, and best of all, meetings, and that you wouldn't even have time to eat lunch? Brilliant!

Most humans weren't built to continuously do the same thing, the same way, at the same time every day. If you don't believe me, talk with someone who spent their entire work life at a drill press in a factory.

We have good days and bad. Some of us work well in the morning while others late at night. Some can work for hours without a break while others get antsy after only 20 minutes.

Having to sit down and force yourself to finish a task when it's the last thing you want to do will not be one of your most productive work moments.

Instead, listen to what your body wants. Follow the flow that's inside of you. Believe me, it's there. Stop working when you get tired or bored. Take a break, take a nap, take a hike. Better yet, keep walking. If you work at home, unload the dryer or the dishwasher. Then when you have caught your breath, jump back in. The quality and amount of work that you will produce when you follow your work flow will astound you.

And now they've gotten rid of recess and gym class at school? Inconceivable!

175

Leave ten minutes earlier for your morning commute.

Would you be willing to throw ten minutes away on your morning commute?

Think about your drive to work. When was the last time you really enjoyed it? For many people, it's simply a race to arrive on time. If that wasn't bad enough, think how you feel when an emergency is thrown at you just as you walk in the door. ("No doctor, no unusual stress. Just the normal day-in-day-out stress that is turning my brain into mush. Why do you ask?")

Imagine how pleasant your drive would be if you had plenty of time and no cares in the world (all right, I am stretching it a bit) as you watch other cars maneuver for position and cut one another off.

By giving yourself those extra ten minutes, you'll actually be able to enjoy your commute and experience the present. Who knows? You may even stop using your smartphone.

You've got to give to get. Ten will get you a lot more later on.

176

When you go on vacation, leave your troubles behind.

Can you leave your work behind when you go on vacation? Not to mention all of your technology too?

Today, your troubles are not only your concerns, issues, and worries, but also your work, brief case, computer, and sometimes even your smartphone.

Vacation comes from the Latin word vacate (at least it sounds pretty good). Vacate not only from your physical premises, but also from your mental ones.

When you're always busy, your life flies by so quickly that you hardly have time to notice you have lost it. Some even classify it as an addiction—no different from a drug, sex, debt, gambling, or eating addiction. Today the scary part is that it's kind of hard to tell that you are addicted when so many others are doing the same thing.

Say it with me, "Vay-cate."

177

Use yellow manila folders for paperwork to work on when traveling.

When traveling, do you use the same paper system you use when working in your office?

One of the goals of the *A Vetter Way*® system is to use the same work system whether you are at the office, at home, or on the road. Both electronically and with paper.

Your electronic (e-mail, smartphone, computer) files and paper files all need to be aligned. Use the same four Action Categories: Batched (Similar items); Calendar (Can only do on a specific date); Projects (A series of steps); and To Do (Important tasks) when you are on the road working with paper.

Print the name of each of the four Action Categories on a separate yellow manila folder. That way, when you travel, you can grab any paper work you want to take along from your four paper Action Categories. Simply pull the work from the same four Action Category (yellow) hanging folders you have in your office.

Sometimes same is good.

178

Pack a box for each specific area when you move.

Remember your last move? Or maybe you'd rather not. After moving, did you discover you had packed more stuff than you had space for in your new location? Not having the space, did the boxes just kind of sit unpacked for a while? Are they still sitting?

The next time you move, scope out your new location listing all rooms and storage places. Then break down each room with the specific area that you will be storing stuff in, such as the closet, a shelf, or a drawer.

Start with your Master Bedroom. Think about the furniture and drawers. Now the closet, shelves and racks. What will go into each of them?

The goal is to come up with a box for each specific shelf, drawer or area. You will need to guesstimate the number of boxes needed for new areas that you didn't have in your old location.

Use the labeling formula: Room/Area/Specific space to identify each box. An example would be: Master Bedroom/Bureau/Top two drawers.

Every box that you move will be labeled with the Room/Area/Specific space it will go into. When you move, simply put each labeled box into its designated room. Open and unload the boxes into their specified area. A perfect fit. Now how did that happen?

♪Off you go, into your wild, blue (and now organized) bedroom.♪

179

Eliminate having to drive in bad traffic.

Are you tired of fighting more and more traffic every day?

Take this quiz to see how you can improve your morning drive. How many do you do?

1. Driving and staying in the left lane instead of using it to pass. (The left lane, believe it or not, is for passing only.)
2. Cutting in front of another car without using your blinker. (Or use your blinker and cut in rather quickly.)
3. Text or check your smartphone while driving. (Make note to self: Mobile use is now the leading cause of death behind the wheel.)
4. Attempt to make a yellow light and don't make it. (It is called going through a red light.)
5. Force your way onto the interstate. Expect the cars that are already driving on it to yield to you. Worse, think you have the right of way. (Uh-oh. You don't.)
6. Wait in the middle of an intersection to turn and then after all of the other cars drive through at the last moment (that are trying to make a yellow light), turn after the light turns red. By the way, this holds up all of the traffic that has a green light the other way. (Add three points for this one.)
7. Leave a large space in front of you at a stoplight so as not to crash into the car in front of you while you check your smartphone. (The guy at the end of the line doesn't have a chance of making the light.)
8. When a truck is stopped or parked in your lane and you need to drive around it, don't wait in your lane until the traffic in the other lane that has the right of way drives through. Rather, gun it and make them wait. (Oh wait. Did you cross over a yellow line?)
9. Drive to the beginning of a long line of cars that are queued up to exit, rather than to the back or end of the line. Then, when someone doesn't let you in. get upset with them, and then aggressively force your way in. Meanwhile you are holding up everyone behind you in your lane. (Add two points for this one.)

10. Never, ever wave Thank You when someone lets you in. This is the Age of Entitlement, isn't it? (Now you know why no one will let you in.)

Score your yesses:

1–3 Yeses: It will be a good to normal ride.
4–5 Yeses: It is going to be a bad traffic day.
6 + Yeses: Do the world a favor and take the bus.

As Pogo said years ago: "We have met the enemy and he is us."

So what kind of drive are you planning on having today?

180

Know where your sales come from.

As a salesperson, do you know where your sales come from? Many don't.

Do this simple exercise:

Go back and list every sale you have made in the last two years. Then to the right of each sale, list how you got it. Was it from a referral? A networking event? Or maybe from a speech, you silver tongued smoothie, you.

Once you have listed how you got each sale, total up each of the various ways.

Now look at each of the ways. Which of the activities resulted in your least sales? Why would you want to spend a lot of time or money on those activities again? Instead, double the time you spend on those activities which produced the most sales.

One last question: Which activity resulted in absolutely no sales at all?

181

Reduce the number of products you sell.

Have you ever eaten at a restaurant with an endless number of menu items?

Think about the logistics needed to serve 100 items. The ordering, receiving and stocking of deliveries, the capital needed for inventory, the training, the personnel, and the knowledge needed to prepare and cook all of the items. Basically, a logistics nightmare.

Now compare that with a restaurant that only has four items. How much easier and cost effective would that operation be?

I remember when McDonalds started many years ago with a limited menu: hamburgers (15 cents), fries, sodas and shakes. After they perfected their work processes, and only when they did, and after establishing a regular customer base, they gradually added more menu items, one at a time, very slowly and deliberately.

How is your operation? Do you have too many items on your menu?

Maybe it is time for a diet.

182

The 80/20 Rule: Your Sales Team.

Which members of your sales team do you spend most of your time with?

80% of your sales team's volume comes from 20% of your team. That means only 20% comes from the other 80% of your team. Yikes!

Are you spending the majority of your time with the 80%, trying to get them to sell more or make them into better salespeople? Most do with the noblest of intentions. I used to.

Or rather, are you focusing on the 20% who are producing the majority of your sales—and will produce a substantial more amount with any kind of attention or assistance.

Your heart is in the right place. Unfortunately, it isn't helping your sales volume—or your wallet.

Somebody stop me...now!

183

Use a checklist form to streamline your work processes.

How many times during the day do you reinvent the wheel when you don't need to?

Instead, create a checklist that lists the steps of your repetitive tasks. The form will remember everything you need to do—so you won't have to.

Set up the checklist numerically by listing major steps with minor steps under the major ones. The goal of the form is to have as many of the possibilities listed as possible so that all you will have to do is check a box ☐ or fill in a date   / /2016.

Example:

☐ 1. Create the plan of operations

    ☐ 1. Set up a list of attendees

    ☐ 2. Prepare the outline for the meeting

    ☐ 3. Call the attendees

        ☐ 1. Left messages   / /2016

            ☐ Everyone called

        ☐ 2. People who aren't coming:

            1.

            2.

            3.

☐ 2. Brainstorm

Not only do you save a lot of time but you also will never miss a step.

184

Lead with the model of having time.

As a leader, how much quality time do you spend sitting around and thinking?

During a session with a Fortune 50 VP of Manufacturing, my client casually mentioned that what he really wanted to do, just once in a while, was look out of the window and spend some quality time thinking and planning. He then stated he couldn't because he didn't have the time.

As I sat there pinching my leg, hoping to awaken myself from this terrifying dream, a wild urge came over me to lean over the desk, shake my client silly and ask him why the heck he thought he couldn't. Sitting in front of me was one of the country's most powerful VPs yet he believed he didn't have time to just sit and think.

If he couldn't make the time, who could in his organization?

The answer, unfortunately, was no one.

Management today simply doesn't feel as if they have the time to work on proactive tasks.

If you aren't working on them, don't be surprised if your people aren't either.

Monkey see, monkey do.

185

Set up a performance review every six months with your employees.

How long does it take you to do a performance review for a new employee? Or rather, do you ever do one?

When a new employee is hired, set up appointments on your calendar to conduct a one, three, six, and twelve-month review with him or her. Employees can't change what they aren't aware of. Neither can they read your mind. No one likes having the boom lowered on them, especially if they haven't been warned.

Reviews can be short and simple. It's a great time to clarify what you expect. It's also a great time to ask for their feedback unless you consistently win Boss of the Year.

So many misunderstandings, resentments, and issues can be resolved if you take this simple action. It just may decrease your turnover.

Who knows? You may actually get what you've always wanted from your employees.

Perish the thought!

186

Your assistant's productivity is directly proportionate to the amount of quality time you spend with that person.

Are you causing your assistant to be unproductive? How many times are they held up from completing something because they need to talk with you and can't—because you are just too busy? Well, excuse you!

Meet with them, or call them if you are traveling (don't e-mail them) three times a day—first thing in the morning, after lunch, and late afternoon. A good time is when they bring in your Inbox contents (if you are one of the lucky ones).

Become accessible. A few minutes invested with them will pay you back tenfold.

If you meet with them, they will produce—a lot more.

187

Manage your employees from a 3 x 5 card.

Do you manage all of your employees the same way or do you consciously approach each one differently?

How many times have any of your bosses asked how you would like to be managed? Wouldn't you work just a little bit harder if they treated you the way you wanted to be treated?

Ask your employees two simple questions—how they want and don't want to be managed. After asking, jot both ways down on a 3 x 5 card. Carry the card with you until you know them by heart. Read the card before interacting with them.

Just nitpick an employee who loves his independence and you'll soon understand the value of doing this—if he's still working for you.

So simple, so effective, yet so few employees are asked.

188

Hire your missing skill.

Do you just like to plan a task or a project, but hate to implement it?

Welcome to the club! It sounds as if you desperately need an Implementer.

Why not hire, contract with, or find someone who is good at what you aren't?

Any shuddering, rapid breathing or sweaty palms while reading the words below are a dead give-away for activities that you need help with.

- Planning
- Implementing
- Researching
- Coordinating

- Selling
- Presenting
- Training
- Accounting

Don't forget that a lot of people love to do what you hate to do. What skill do you need to find that will make you a lot happier... and even more productive?

Hire it, rent it, buy it, or beg for it as fast as you can. Then notice how much more work you get done now that you are doing what you really like to do.

189

Cut all the dotted lines above below you in an org chart except one.

What do you call it when your employees have three bosses all wanting something done immediately? A normal day?

Quite simply, the more people your employees have to you answer to, the greater the odds of their being bombarded with urgent tasks. The more urgent tasks thrown at them by more than one manager, the less chance they will have of working on anything remotely important.

The ideal number of people to report to: One.

You are probably going to have to ask Santa Claus for this one unless he happens to be your boss.

190

Ask each of your employees what their Priority is.

If you asked your employees what their priority was, would their answer be the same as yours?

Write down each of your employee's priority. Notice priority is singular—not plural. Then ask each of your employees to write down what they think their priority is. A priority is an activity that when focused on and done, causes everything else to fall into its proper place. Compare what you have written with what they have written. Oh-boy!

Ninety-nine out of 100 times, two very different descriptions will occur. And some bosses wonder why their employees aren't doing what they want.

Surprise! It may be time to talk.

191

Set up a job description around a person.

Why do you procrastinate on certain tasks at work? Could it be because you hate doing them, or aren't very good at them?

Your job came with a preset list of responsibilities that you were qualified to do. Perhaps qualified, but a desire to do them? Hardly.

No matter how well a job candidate is selected, many times, parts of their job are procrastinated causing a slowdown for the entire group. Yet, we continue to try to fit a square peg into a round hole with how we hire around preset job duties.

Why not create a job around what someone is good at (skilled) or likes to do?

When a football team drafts a top passer, do they continue to run, or do they change to a passing game?

Maybe it is time for your team to go down and long. Real long.

192

Hire someone who likes to change.

Do you like to change?

Surprisingly, many people say they do. I am not so sure. After 25 years in the change business what may be truer is: "I like change... as long as it's someone else who is doing the changing."

Years ago when I was running a 36 million dollar telecommunications region, most people were hiring workers who had experience. Not me. I was hiring people with an attitude—a great attitude. With the right attitude, I could train them to be top salespeople.

Today if I were hiring, not only would a great attitude be needed, but more importantly, a willingness to change. Why? Because brothers and sisters, we are knee deep in change and the river, it is arising with even more change.

The next time you are ready to hire someone, ask them if they like to change. When they say yes, ask them to name five things that they successfully changed in the last year. Believe me. That will be one interesting story.

"Change? We don't need no stinkin' change."

Maybe we do.

193

Have your interviewee show you.

Have you ever hired the wrong admin? Was it because they said they could perform a task in the interview and you later found out they couldn't? But how could you have really known for sure?

Have them perform the task for you.

Interviews are about asking questions, checking references, and getting a sense of compatibility. Then, having everyone talk with them so no one gets blamed for a poor hire.

How will you know that they are able to do what you need them to do? Because they did it in another job with another boss? Are you really willing to trust that?

An example would be to ask them what organizational system they use. Ask them to thoroughly explain how it works (boy will you be surprised at what they say). Next, give them an admin problem and ask them to explain, step by step, how they would handle it (better yet, have them show you). Then give them a computer task and ask them to do it (actually watch them). The task needs to be what you will expect them to do in their job.

There is nothing more valuable than watching someone actually do what they are supposed to be doing before you hire them. Unfortunately, few people hire this way.

Your turnover rate will drop if you hire this way.

194

Stop the meetings.

How much time have you wasted in your life going to meetings? Who keeps calling these things anyway?

Try something different. Make a decision on your own. Stop playing the CYA game. Stop asking upper management to sit in so you can show them how much you know. They don't want to be in a meeting any more than you do. Take a chance. Allow your subordinates some room to fail once in a while when they take the initiative.

Most importantly, stop having so many meetings. Yeah, I'm talking to you.

Just one time, do the math on the money you spend on salaries for just one meeting.

You want your bottom line and stock price to go up? Stop going to meetings and get some work done for a change.

Stop the madness.

195

The best facilitator for a meeting is someone other than the boss.

Isn't it kind of intimidating when your boss runs a meeting? You don't always feel like jumping right in and telling her that she is wrong when she asks your opinion about something, do you?

When a trained facilitator runs the show, meetings begin and end on time, there's more closure, more accountability, and more follow-up.

Bosses don't always possess the skills needed to facilitate. In fact, a lot of times they really don't possess the skills at all. Using someone else in the group frees them up to participate and contribute—something the facilitator shouldn't be doing.

Hey! All you bosses out there. Please, take a seat and let someone else run the show—or at least the meeting for a change.

Notice what happens to the number of meetings that are called when this occurs.

196

Use meetings for decision-making and brainstorming.

Why do you need to have a meeting and go over what you just sent out by e-mail?

Many people feel the need to use a meeting as a way to disperse information. Hello! We're living in the middle of the Digital Age or whatever Age we are in now with a gazillion ways to distribute information. A meeting is not the way to do it anymore.

Send the information ahead of time and let them be responsible for reading it. Use the meeting for brainstorming and decision-making only.

Isn't repeating what was sent out and read, redundant and a waste of time?

The "Department of Redundancy Department" strikes again and again.

197

Stand during meetings.

Do you enjoy going to meetings? Do you know anyone that does? On the other hand, there are always the doughnuts.

Quite simply, the goal of most sane people is to spend less time in meetings and more time getting work accomplished.

The group will never allow anyone to ramble on when everyone is standing. When you stand during a meeting, two things will occur. One, people will get to the point rather quickly, and two, oddly enough, fewer meetings will be called. What a shame!

Now get rid of those chairs and start making some decisions!

198

Standardize how you store information throughout your company.

Are you aware that eventually your company will have to standardize how it stores information? You think you are getting a lot of information now? Give it a few years.

By standardizing how you store and access information, all of your employees will be able to use the same system regardless of where the information comes from. This includes all paper, computer, and e-mail, as well as shared, departmental, and central files.

When someone is out sick, on vacation, taking maternity leave, or on the road, anyone in the office will be able to retrieve information instantly from that person's desk, computer or shared drive. New employees won't have to reinvent the wheel—a system will already be in place so they can begin Producing almost immediately. For employees who are fired, forced to leave (nicely called downsizing today), or quit, you will be able to access and understand their information system and what they have been working on in seconds. In the near future, every company will be forced to do this to survive the onslaught of information that is yet to come.

As the BTO song goes: ♫You ain't seen nothing yet!♫

199

Combine as many forms as possible into one form.

Is the same information duplicated on more than one of your forms?

Questions to ask your forms (if they could answer and even wanted to):

- Who created you?
- How long ago were you created?
- What is your purpose?
- How often do I use you?
- Can I combine pieces of you with other forms to make one form?
- Do you ask for information that I no longer need or use?
- Sorry about this one but… can I eliminate you?

Hint: When talking to your forms, do it with your door closed. If they answer back, it may be time to change jobs.

200

Repair a Microsoft Office problem.

Do you ever see rotating circles on your screen when using a Microsoft program such as Word or Outlook? How about pink elephants after a night on the town?

Problem: Rotating circles

Solution: Do a Quick Repair.

1. In Windows 7, left click the round Start button on the bottom left of your screen on your Taskbar.

2. A pop-up menu will pop up.
3. Find Control Panel on the right hand side and left click on it.
4. A new page will open with icons on it.
5. Find Programs and Features and left click on it to open it.
6. A new page will open with a listing of all of the programs you have on your computer.
7. Find the Microsoft Office software program that you use such as Microsoft Office Home and Business 2013.
8. Right click on it.
9. A dialogue box will open up with two options, Uninstall and Change.
10. Click on Change.
11. A dialogue box will open with two options, Quick Repair and Online Repair.
12. Click on Quick Repair.
13. On the bottom of the page, click on the Repair button.

Problem: Seeing pink elephants

Solution: Stop drinking so much and stay home once in a while.

Great! Now that you have saved money from not needing a computer repair visit, you can go out on the town and celebrate.

Uh-oh!

201

Fix the process.

Does it ever feel as if you are getting blamed for something that isn't your fault? Especially around review time?

In most organizations, many problems are caused by faulty systems or processes, not faulty people. To create a successful, smooth-running operation, you must separate the process from the people. Or is it the people from the process?

Processes are comprised of a series of actions designed to create a result. All work is a process, although many workers don't think of it that way.

Don't add people in order to fix the problem.

Instead, simply fix the process.

Appendix 1
GLOSSARY

Action	Anything you intend to work on or do, now or in the future. Everything you keep in or out of your office, both electronic and paper, is either an Action or a Support (Save).
Category	A grouping of similar or like items. Categories are broken down by a subject. There are both Action and Support Categories. Categories are used for both electronic and paper storage of information. The key is to ask "What is it?"
FADS	The only four places information can go from your e-mail Inbox: Forward, Action, Delete, Support (Save).
Files	Both Action and Support Categories are made up of these. Support Categories can either be electronic/paper (in a hanging folder) or non-paper items (on a shelf or in a drawer).
OATS	The only four places information can go from your desk Inbox: Out Box, Action, Trash, Support (Save).
Processing	The sorting, prioritizing and categorizing of all of your information. No work is accomplished when you Process information. You Process your e-mail Inbox, your voice mail, your desk Inbox, your smartphone, and any other incoming information.
Producing	Creating results and accomplishing work. Never Process and Produce at the same time (multitasking).
Quiet Time	This is your most important time of your day. Your day needs to revolve around

	this time. It is 20% of your workday that is completely uninterrupted. Take your QT at the same time every day. Work on your 1-5's in your QT.
Reference Category	A Support Category which includes miscellaneous files that don't easily fit into any of your other Support Categories. All Support Categories originate from your Reference Category.
Support	Any information that you refer to. You have no intention of doing anything with Support items or working on them. Support Categories can be either electronic/paper or non-paper.
Windows Explorer	This is where you store all of your non-Action information that you want to save and refer to. You will have twelve or fewer Support Categories (folders).

Greg Vetter

Appendix 2

THE BIG PICTURE

**Everything you work on goes into Action.
All information you save goes into Support**

OUTLOOK	WINDOWS EXPLORER
OR	OR
HANGING FOLDER	**HANGING FOLDER**
ACTION (tasks to do)	SUPPORT (saved info)
This is where you work from. Everything you need to work on is in here.	This is where you store all of your information you want to save.
4 Action Categories	12< Support Categories

Appendix 3
PROCESSING AND PRODUCING

**Process information three times a day.
Produce work three times a day.**

PROCESSING (Information)

Daily

- **Three (3) times a day go through your:**
  - E-mail Inbox
  - Voice mail
  - Desk Inbox
  - Smartphone

Weekly

- **Once (1) a week**

On the last day of the week, review all of your four Action Category files. This allows you an awareness of what needs to be done and an opportunity to set up the following week's tasks and activities.

PRODUCING (Work)

Daily

- **Once a day, work from each of the following three Action Categories:**

  - **Calendar** – Work on those tasks that must be and can only be done on a specific date.

  - **Batched** – Work on similar type tasks in the same time period. Think assembly line work.

  - **To Do** – Important and impactful tasks. Tasks that you can do before they are due. Steps from a Project. Work on these tasks in your Quiet Time (QT).

Appendix 4
ACTION AND SUPPORT

Everything in your office is either an Action or a Support.

KINETIC ENERGY

Properties of an Action:

- Activity
- Task
- Verb
- Intend to do... now or in the future

POTENTIAL ENERGY

Properties of a Support:

- Something you refer to
- A resource
- Saved information
- No intention of doing anything with it

Appendix 5
SUPPORT CATEGORIES IN WINDOWS EXPLORER

You can have twelve or fewer Support Categories.

- 📁 Desktop
  - 📁 Libraries
    - 📁 Documents
      - 📁 My Documents (below are examples of Support Categories)
        - 📁 Clients
        - 📁 Computer
        - 📁 Finances
        - 📁 Forms
        - 📁 Graphics
        - 📁 Literature
        - 📁 Personal
        - 📁 PR
        - 📁 Productivity issues
        - 📁 Products
        - 📁 Reference
        - 📁 Services

Appendix 6
FADS

From your e-mail Inbox, e-mails only go to one of four places:

FADS (Forward, Action, Delete, Support)

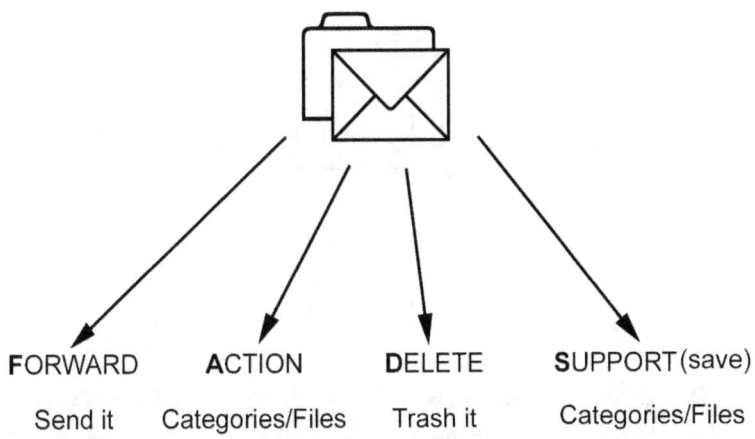

FORWARD   **A**CTION   **D**ELETE   **S**UPPORT (save)

Send it   Categories/Files   Trash it   Categories/Files

Appendix 7
OATS

From your desk Inbox, there are only four places information can go:

OATS (Outbox, Action, Trash, Support)

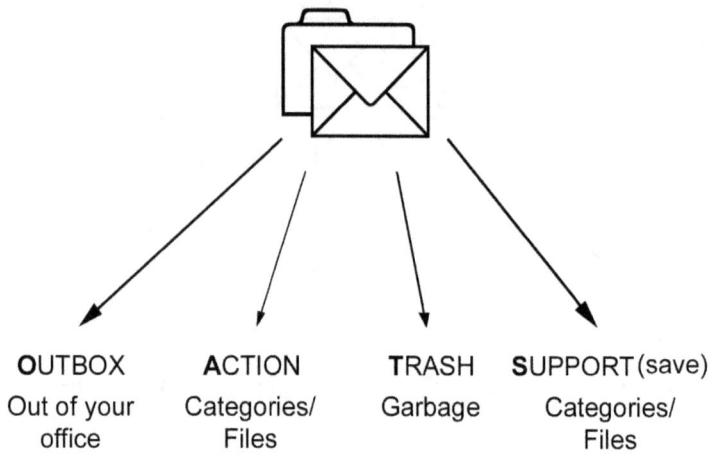

OUTBOX	**A**CTION	**T**RASH	**S**UPPORT (save)
Out of your office	Categories/ Files	Garbage	Categories/ Files

Appendix 8
ACTION CATEGORIES

There are four Action Categories.

TO DO	CALENDAR
AN IMPORTANT TASK DONE IN YOUR QT	CAN ONLY BE DONE TODAY A SPECIFIC DATE OR MONTH
PROJECTS	**BATCHED**
TASKS THAT CAN BE BROKEN DOWN INTO STEPS	SIMILAR TASKS THAT ARE WORKED ON AT THE SAME TIME

Appendix 9
ACTION CATEGORIES IN YOUR E-MAIL

Your four Action Category folders go under your Inbox folder.

- Inbox
  - **_Batched** (Similar tasks)
    - Call
    - Data Entry
    - E-mail
    - Left message
    - Read
    - Reply
    - Sent E-mail
    - Talk with
      - Elaine (optional)
      - Jack (optional)
  - **_Calendar** (Date)
    - Pending (Waiting for something from others without a specified date)
      - Direct reports (optional)
        - Elaine (optional)
        - Jack (optional)
      - Proposals (optional)

    (1-31 and Jan-Dec are in your e-mail program calendar)

  - **_Projects** (A series of steps to do over a period of time)
    - The Project Name (A Guide Sheet that provides an overview goes here)
      - Steps (Each separate task to do)
      - Support (Any non-action information can be temporarily stored here)

  - **_To Do** (Important Tasks)
    - 1-5 (Your top 5 To Do A tasks you work on in your Quiet Time)
    - A (Very Important)
    - B (Important)
    - C (Somewhat Important)

Appendix 10
5 STEPS OF YOUR E-MAIL INBOX

Your Inbox will be completely emptied after Processing it.

1. **Stand**. Stand up. It is a lot quicker than sitting down.

2. **Ask FADS**. Ask yourself whether the item is a Forward, Action, Delete or Support (save).

3. **Decide the Category**. If the item is an Action (a task) or a Support (information to save), decide the Category name and the File name you will drag it to.

4. **Use all of your senses**. Say the five steps out loud. For example, "Stand, Support, Financial, Budget." Hear yourself say it, see it and touch it. The more senses you use when going through your Inbox, the greater the chance you will have of remembering where you stored it.

5. **File it away**. Drag the message to the folder or file location you want.

Appendix 11

5 STEPS OF YOUR DESK INBOX

Your Inbox will be completely emptied after Processing it.

1. **Stand**. Stand up. It is a lot quicker than sitting down.

2. **Ask OATS**. Ask yourself whether the item is an Outbox, Action, Trash or Support (save).

3. **Decide the Category**. If the item is an Action (a task) or a Support (information to save), decide the Category name and the File name you will move it to.

4. **Use all of your senses**. Say the five steps out loud. For example, "Stand, Support, Financial, Budget." Hear yourself say it, see it and touch it. The more senses you use when going through your Inbox, the greater the chance you will have of remembering where you stored it.

5. **File it away**. Move the document to the folder you want.

Greg Vetter

Appendix 12
HOW THE *A VETTER WAY*® SYSTEM WORKS

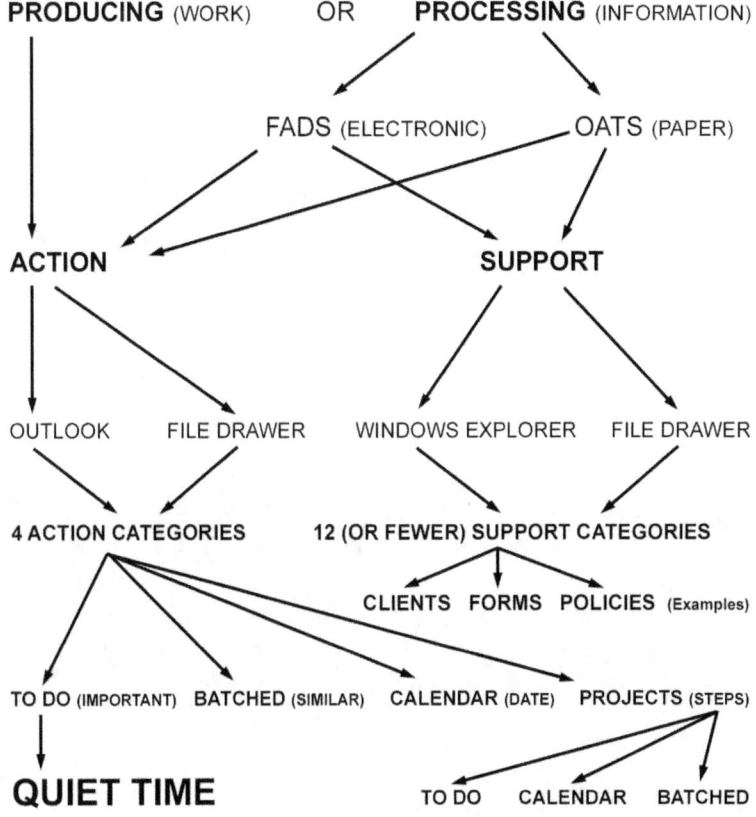

About the Author

Greg Vetter is President of Vetter Productivity, an organizational training and consulting firm founded in Atlanta in 1989 and author of the book, *Find It In 5 Seconds-Gaining Control In The Information Age*.

Greg creates systems and work processes that allow you to work smarter, faster and more efficiently—that is, produce more in less time and with less stress. More importantly, he gives you back control of your work life. He does this through speeches, workshops, executive focus coaching, consulting, and licensing his organizational system, *A Vetter Way*®.

Greg's services differ from those of the typical time-management company. He doesn't fall for the easy answer, but searches for the motivation behind why people do what they do. Feeling overwhelmed or out of control, drowning in clutter, and reacting constantly to interruptions are symptoms, not causes, of deeper psychological issues. By resolving these issues, people are free to work at their peak capacity.

Greg has created many systems and work processes including space and design layout for a printing company; streamlining the workflow and storage system for chemists in a lab for Coca-Cola; creating a location shoot work flow system for a CNN producer, and standardizing a company's entire information system.

Greg studied Psychology and was graduated from the University of Dubuque. From boyhood on, he grew up and worked in his family's construction business. He worked in various psychology-related positions before entering the restaurant industry. He started and operated his own restaurant and catering business in Atlanta. As a District Sales Manager in the telecommunications industry, he developed and ran a $36 million sales territory where his sales representatives were consistently ranked in the top ten nationally.

Products
A VETTER WAY® LEARNING SERIES

- **Books**
  - Find It In 5 Seconds - Gaining Control In The Information Age
- **Workbooks**
  - *A Vetter Way*® To Work in the 21st Century
  - *A Vetter Way*® To Gain Control of your E-mail and Computer Files
- **CDs**
  - Winning The Productivity Game - 201 Time-Saving Solutions To Work Smarter, Faster and Easier

Programs

Greg Vetter
Speaker • Trainer • Coach

The perfect choice for a highly interactive,
fun, and content-packed program.

Speeches

- Gaining Control Of Your E-mail And Computer Files
- Shredding The Organizational Myths Of The Workplace
- Twelve Things You Should Never, Ever Do With E-mail

Workshops and Group Hands-on Training

- *A Vetter Way*® To Gain Control Of Your E-mail And Computer Files
- *A Vetter Way*® To Work in the 21st Century
- *A Vetter Way*® To Standardize Your Information
- *A Vetter Way*® To Eliminate Your Gray Areas
- *A Vetter Way*® To Lead Productive Meetings

One-on-ones

- Executive Focus Coaching
- Organizational (Office, paper, e-mail, computer, and smartphone)

To order any of these products or for more information contact Greg Vetter at:

Phone: 404-250-1727

E-mail: greg@vetterproductivity.com

Web page: www.vetterproductivity.com

www.ingramcontent.com/pod-product-compliance
Lightning Source LLC
Chambersburg PA
CBHW050638300426
44112CB00012B/1855